D0008399

Religion in
American Public Life

THE AMERICAN ASSEMBLY was established by Dwight D. Eisenhower at Columbia University in 1950. Each year it holds at least two nonpartisan meetings that give rise to authoritative books that illuminate issues of United States policy.

An affiliate of Columbia, the Assembly is a national, educational institution incorporated in the state of New York.

The Assembly seeks to provide information, stimulate discussion, and evoke independent conclusions on matters of vital public interest.

THE AMERICAN ASSEMBLY
Columbia University

Religion in American Public Life

Living with Our Deepest Differences

Azizah Y. al-Hibri
Jean Bethke Elshtain
Charles C. Haynes
Introduction by Martin E. Marty

W. W. Norton & Company
New York • London

Copyright © 2001 by The American Assembly

All rights reserved
Printed in the United States of America
First Edition

For information about permission to reproduce selections from this book,
write to Permissions, W. W. Norton & Company, Inc.,
500 Fifth Avenue, New York, NY 10110

The text and display of this book are composed in Baskerville.
Composition by Allentown Digital Services Division of
R.R. Donnelley & Sons Company
Manufacturing by Haddon Craftsmen, Inc.

Library of Congress Cataloging-in-Publication Data

Hibri, Azizah, 1943–
Religion in American public life : living with our deepest differences / Azizah Y.
al-Hibri, Jean Bethke Elshtain, Charles C. Haynes ; introduction by Martin E. Marty.
p. cm.
At head of title: The American Assembly, Columbia University.
Includes bibliographical references and index.
ISBN 0-393-32206-8 (pbk.)
1. United States—Religion. I. Elshtain, Jean Bethke, 1941– II. Hayes,
Charles C. III. American Assembly. IV. Title.

BL2525.H53 2001
200'.973—dc21   2001024008

W. W. Norton & Company, Inc., 500 Fifth Avenue, New York, N.Y. 10110
www.wwnorton.com

W. W. Norton & Company Ltd., Castle House,
75/76 Wells Street, London W1T 3QT

1 2 3 4 5 6 7 8 9 0

Contents

Preface

The American Assembly commissioned this volume as part of its multi-year series entitled *Uniting America: Toward Common Purpose*, a project designed to help reverse some of the most difficult and divisive forces in our society. This book was for the second Assembly in the *Uniting America* series, which focused on "Matters of Faith: The Role of Religion in American Public Life."

This Assembly sought to identify as wide a circle as possible of shared values among the many religions in the United States concerning how to manage their differences in the public square. It was designed to engender an atmosphere of mutual respect in public life in which their religious differences could be discussed in a less divisive way and in which those shared values could help resolve nonreligious issues, and thus lead toward a more united America.

Among the specific issues addressed were the following:

- How should we address religion in public education?
- How should the First Amendment guarantees apply to current controversies concerning religion in public life?
- Should state-religious institution partnerships be encouraged?

- How should we live with our differences on such issues as sexual orientation, abortion, and physician-assisted suicide?
- What role should religion play in business and corporate governance, not for profit organizations, academia, citizen action, and science and technology?

The book opens with an introductory chapter by Martin E. Marty, director of the Public Religion Project and professor, University of Chicago, who chaired this Assembly as well as a distinguished Leadership Council for the project. The council consisted of fourteen leaders of major religions in the United States, who helped to provide guidance. (Their names are listed at the end of this book.) The co-directors for this Assembly and authors of three individual chapters were Azizah Y. al-Hibri, professor, T.C. Williams School of Law, University of Richmond; Jean Bethke Elshtain, professor, University of Chicago Divinity School; and Charles C. Haynes, senior scholar, the Freedom Forum First Amendment Center. Additionally, the book contains a "charge" (memo urging action) from the chair to the participants and the text of an address to the participants by Os Guinness of the Trinity Forum.

Drafts of the chapters in this volume were used as background for an Assembly of fifty-seven leaders from American government, business, labor, law, academia, nonprofit organizations, the media, and different religious faiths and faith based organizations who gathered at Arden House, Harriman, New York, for the Ninety-sixth American Assembly, March 23–26, 2000. For three days the participants worked together to define policies and actions concerning the role of religion in American public life.

Following their discussions, the participants issued a report of their findings and recommendations. The text of the report is included in this book and is also available on The American Assembly's website (www.americanassembly.org or AOL keyword AmericanAssembly), along with information about other Assembly programs.

The American Assembly *Uniting America* series commenced with an Assembly on economic growth and opportunity (June 10–13, 1999), and resulted in the publication of the book *Updating America's Social Contract: Economic Growth and Opportunity in the New Century* by economists Rudolph G. Penner, Isabel V. Sawhill, and Timothy Taylor. Other topics addressed in the overall series include family as the core unit of society (September 21–24, 2000), racial divisions (April 19–22, 2001), and improving intersector cooperation among business, government, and the nonprofit world (civil society) and citizens necessary to help move our society toward common purpose in the twenty-first century (fall 2001). A distinguished national Leadership Advisory Group helped to design this series, and will convene toward the end of 2001, after the fifth Assembly, to issue its own overview report of the principal findings and recommendations from the entire series. This leadership group is co-chaired by three trustees of The American Assembly, David R. Gergen, Karen Elliott House, and Donald F. McHenry, and by Paul H. O'Neill, chairman of ALCOA Inc. (A list of the members of the Leadership Advisory Group can be found at the end of this volume.) This series will undertake not only to make the necessary recommendations, but will also develop action plans and follow-on activities necessary to achieve the policy recommendations.

The American Assembly gratefully acknowledges those funders whose generous support helped make this book and the project on religion in public life possible:

The Goizueta Foundation
The Ford Foundation
Lilly Endowment, Inc.
The Henry Luce Foundation, Inc.

As this Assembly is part of The American Assembly series *Uniting America,* our appreciation is also expressed to those who have funded the series overall or a portion thereof:

The Ford Foundation
Hallmark Corporate Foundation
The McKnight Foundation
Surdna Foundation, Inc.
The Coca-Cola Company
Robert W. Woodruff Foundation
Ewing Marion Kauffman Foundation
Foundation for Child Development

Walter and Elise Haas Fund
Xerox Corporation
Bradley Currey, Jr.
Annie E. Casey Foundation
WEM Foundation
Robert Abernethy
Genuine Parts Company
King & Spalding
Herman Russell
SunTrust Banks, Inc.
Wachovia Bank
Eleanor B. Sheldon

As in all of our publications, the policy views expressed in this volume are those of its authors, and do not necessarily reflect the views of The American Assembly, nor its funders or participants.

It is our hope and belief that this volume and the future Assemblies in the *Uniting America* series will help to stimulate a constructive national dialogue in the United States that will contribute toward a more united America.

Daniel A. Sharp
President and CEO
The American Assembly

Religion in
American Public Life

Introduction:
Faith Matters

Martin E. Marty

W hat is the matter with American public life that leads three scholars and The American Assembly to produce this volume? What possibly can "religion" have to do with the matter? Religion, many Americans still say, is "a private affair." Religious and nonreligious people alike find reason to keep it away from the public scene. Some fear that making religion public will taint and corrupt religion, debasing it so that it loses the power to console, ennoble, and inform individuals, even when they congregate. Oth-

MARTIN E. MARTY is the Fairfax M. Cone Distinguished Professor Emeritus at the University of Chicago, the George B. Caldwell Senior Scholar-in-Residence at the Park Ridge Center for Health, Faith, and Ethics, and editor of *Second Opinion*. Ordained into the ministry in 1952, he served for a decade as a Lutheran parish pastor. He has received the National Medal of Humanities, the medal of the American Academy of Arts and Sciences, the University of Chicago Alumni Medal, and the National Book Award. He has been elected to the American Philosophical Society, the American Academy of Political and Social Science, the Society of American Historians, and the American Antiquarian Society. Mr. Marty holds sixty-four honorary doctorates and is the author of fifty books, including three volumes of *Modern American Religion*. He chairs The American Assembly Religion Leadership Council.

ers fear that such "religiocifying" of the public sphere will befoul it and lead to unnecessary new conflicts.

This book begins with the recognition that, whatever some of the pious and more of the secular-minded might prefer, faith, spirituality, and religion are *not* only private affairs. The instinct that led Americans to coin the "private affair" image resulted from many good instincts and had salutary dimensions. Those who migrated to America and set up political institutions here were well aware of religious wars, holy wars, such as those between Christians and Muslims in the Crusades and among Christians and Christians in the Thirty Years' War, the Puritan Revolution, and countless more. Why import religion in forms that could inspire such wars? Why not keep religion boxed in, away from public influence and scrutiny?

The problem with the answers long given to such questions is that religion as a matter of fact has always been a part of American public life. In the way knowledge and power are organized, many elites were distanced from this fact, and lacked perspective or curiosity to make sense of it. Study of religion was rare in higher education, and rarely pursued fairly until a half century ago. Mass media tended to slight or distort religion when it showed up in the public sphere. In voluntary associations and clubs not promoted by religious movements participants found it valuable to downplay religion.

No more. As America grows ever more pluralist in fact and outlook, paradoxically the sight and voice of religion are more evident. When America was dominated by white Protestant male leadership, as it tended to be until the 1950s, everyone else seemed to be in the minority or marginal, and many found it advisable not to risk exposure by dealing with religion in public. After World War II, when a kind of social parity began to appear among Protestants, Catholics, and Jews, there were wary but celebratory explorations concerning religion in public life. But they were often limited. In 1954 Congress added "under God" to the Pledge of Allegiance to the flag. Presidents, beginning with Dwight Eisenhower, began to go public about their faith. But still the moves were tentative, partial, not representative.

To take one illustration of catalytic agencies that brought about change, one points to the African-American churches. Overlooked in the early Protestant-Catholic-Jew reckoning, African-American churches were discovered to be representing the soul of the rural South and the inner city everywhere. These churches showed less concern for the borders between religion and the public life, the separation of church and state, and the like. They first "got away with" welfare policies that were friendly to government and later helped provide new models congruent with the U. S. Constitution for seeing the "faith based" enterprises grow until by 2000 both political parties were advocates.

From these paragraphs it should be clear already that The American Assembly and the authors of this book do not equate "public" with "political." Public is the genus and politics the very important species. Religion certainly shows up in politics in our time, as the use and misuse of it in the 2000 presidential and congressional campaigns made clear. But the law, as embodied in regulations concerning 501(c)(3) charitable agencies, including churches and synagogues, and monitored by the Internal Revenue Service, is an inhibitor against too much direct political expression by religious forces. And many in them practice restraint about politics, in part because they are themselves internally divided on partisan lines.

So one looks elsewhere as well as in the political sphere to see where *Matters of Faith* make their appearance in the public zones. These include schools, voluntary associations, town meetings, the mall, the marketplace, the gallery, the symphony hall, the university, and more. They show up most where what Alexis de Tocqueville, quoted by Jean Bethke Elshtain here, called "the habits of the heart." And they cannot easily be restrained or suppressed. But they can easily be misused.

What's the problem?

In the late 1960s, "after Selma" and shortly before his assassination, the Reverend Martin Luther King, Jr., and his allies tried to bring their nonviolent approaches to bear on racial segregation in housing, education, and jobs in Chicago. Some of their councils were interracial, and I was among the whites who on occasion sat in on planning sessions. Used to patterns in which one plots for years before holding a conference, relying on think tanks and surveys, securing the best academic talent available, we were often startled to see the direct approach of the many "reverends" who led the civil rights movement, at least in this expression.

How do you bring about change? How deal with problems on the racial scene? How promote the common good in the modern metropolis? The answers ran against our patterning instincts. One of King's associates described his technique like this:

First you get a great big hall, probably in a church. Then you get as many people as you can to come into it and sit down in circles. Then you tell them, "Don't any of you come out until you've got the solution!" Someone will ask, "What's the problem?" We'd tell them: "You start talking and you'll know what the problem is."

That approach has its merits and tends to work in some circumstances. For example, in Chicago at that time the focus was very clear: patterns of real estate transaction, "red-lining," "block-busting," and the like hampered efforts to improve public education, safety, and the development of level playing fields among job hunters and job holders. Get people into a room and they would deal with such problems immediately.

When talking about "the common good" or a healthy "American public life" and the role of religion in it, one can learn from but not rely on the technique we heard about then and there. American pluralism deals with hundreds of religious movements, thousands of nongovernmental organizations and other voluntary associations, and myriad governmental agencies from local school boards to the U. S. Supreme Court. Grievances get expressed one way by "ordinary folk" and another by theorists about the public order. Subtle philosophies compete for the mind and bold strategies for the bodies and hearts of citizens.

To have a meaningful conversation, then, there must be some resort to "usual patterns." Thus, to some extent, The American Assembly would be classified as a think tank. It makes no secret of the fact that it wants to draw on top talent, and its leaders even have the courage to admit that they are aiming for those who have their say in policy making and interpreting American life. They do make advance studies—this book was born as an element in a particular experiment, part of a series they call *Uniting America: Toward Common Purpose.* The American Assembly relies on a specialized process to find consensus on public policy issues, and a company of experts on religion found that it works, even among people who expected there would be little. The Assembly develops ways to help perpetuate concerns engendered by an initiative, and this book is intended to be part of such an advance.

At a crucial stage, however, for all the differences, there are analogous experiences in The American Assembly approach. While it does not rent a large hall, it does gather significant and representative people and asks them to "start talking." To be sure that they do talk about many of the same things, the planners narrow some of the possible agenda topics that fit under categories such as "religion," "American," "public," and "life." They do the filtering and focusing through complicated preliminary processes that turn out to be fateful. Guess wrong about "the problems" and you will fail to produce even the beginning of address to "solutions." One thinks of Reinhold Niebuhr's famous reminder that there is nothing more useless than an answer to an unasked question.

This book is about several of the key questions.

First, the initiative behind the book and this Assembly and its outcomes had to deal with the "problem" of religion turned from private to private/public, and had to find ways to do such dealing.

Second, there had to be some analysis of "American public life." This analysis suggested that religion could not be an agent producing "articles of faith" but it could promote "articles of peace"—I am quoting Father John Courtney Murray from Charles C. Haynes's chapter in this book. That is, it would be pretentious and futile to put central theological and religious philosophical tenets on the table. There are said to be 25,000 or more Christian denominations in the world, and almost 250 in the United States. They would not be separate if they could agree on theology and belief. What they have not begun to solve in hundreds of years no trio of authors or set of threescore Assembly participants could touch unless they had gone mad.

While public life positions are grounded in separate theologies, philosophies, worldviews, and communions, however, they can find many constructive things about which to talk to promote the common good.

What else is the matter? What's the problem? In this case again, public imagery has to be taken into account, imagery that is by no means all inaccurate and unfounded. That impression or stereotype issues in the observation that if there is conflict marked by incivility that disrupts efforts to address the common good, introducing the voice of religion or, better, religions, only makes it worse. In such an observation, faith communities bring more heat than light. What has been called *odium theologicum,* the peculiar and passionate form of hatred among thinkers in faith communities devoted to reconciliation, shalom, peace, is rather harmless when it is confined to the echo chambers called seminaries and sanctuaries. But let it appear in the public sphere, and temperatures will rise along with voices.

There is enough truth to such an observation that anyone who would address the urgent topic of religion in public life has to reckon with it. Let health care systems and their ethical panels address issues like *in vitro* fertilization, abortion, or euthanasia, and they will get only so far until they deal with the religious dimensions. They cannot do so effectively without listening to the religious voices. Then talks break down.

Let educators debate sex education, "values clarification," moral formation, and the like. They will soon demonstrate that they have enough over which to disagree. Then let strong advocates and opponents appear at school board meetings to state their case for their version of sex education or no version, and the meeting is likely to break up early.

Invite some religious representatives to be chaplains of public institutions and you invite attack from slighted others. Have a foundation or endowment make grants to religious groups that have denominational names and the other denominations will get angry. (Not true, say veteran observers, but believed in any case by foundations that back off from such consideration of faith communities and their public service). Let presidential candidates testify to their "born again" experience, or misstep in ways that offend religious groups, and they may have to learn expensive, finally defeating lessons.

None of these stereotypes is completely accurate; some are dated; others reflect experiences that have not profited from experiments like the one relating to this book. Yet one must deal with them.

Are we overplaying the conflictual element in religion here? Isn't there another stereotype out there, one that says religion is too passive, bland, boring to have public effect? Most of what goes on under the steeples, towers, domes seems irrelevant to the public that is not a member of the communities gathered under them. Who's afraid of all those congregations in the phone book's Yellow Pages? Who takes hope from them, when the eye is on public concerns?

Over forty years ago my first book on religion and American public life, *The New Shape of American Religion*, "did well," or well enough to attract the notice of one of the primeval talk show hosts, David Susskind, who staged "Open End." On one Sunday night he invited a half dozen of us—Protestant, Catholic, Jew, Agnostic, etc.—to come to New York for open-ended conversation. His agent clearly invited us to deal with "Religion in American Life." That morning the *New York Times* advertised the program, him, and our names. But now the topic was *Fear and Prejudice in the United States*.

The program opened with young William F. Buckley, Jr., prompted by the rest of us, asking why the host changed the name of the program. Susskind had a quick answer ready, an answer born out of staff planning sessions. "If we made it 'Religion in America,' half the people wouldn't tune in because religion is too bland and boring. And the other half wouldn't because it's too controversial and they don't want to be stirred up." (In those days "talk shows" were not yet of the "firing line" sort; we were all more genteel.) So "Fear and Prejudice" sounded exciting enough to lure the one-half of the potential audience, and if the religious dimension got too heated, the host could back off and say we are really talking only about fear and prejudice in general.

Fortunately, forty years later some ways are emerging to avoid the extremes Susskind feared in respect to audience, and there are more efficient means to attract the energy and voices of people who can transcend polarities and seek fresh addresses to advance the common good. But these experiments are still in an early stage.

What will become clear in this book is that no one enters the new conversations or dialogues picturing that everything will be solved. No one expects or even asks people of deep commitments to abandon them. Do not picture the three authors of this book anticipating conversions—to whatever. "Oh, thanks for inviting me to this dialogue. I've been pro-life all my life, but now that I've met you and heard you, I am switching sides and moving to the pro-choice camp." Never. Or almost never. And hardly ever because the intention of the dialogue was not to lead to such conversion.

The authors of this book have too much respect for people of faith who are profoundly convicted, thoughtful, tested, and dedicated to their faith and to one side in contested issues. Given that, they ask, in effect, "But even so, what then?" Is America to be nothing but a collection of self-contained, boundaried enclaves of people who have only their separate stories, positions, conclusions, and causes? Or can some of the resources of the very faiths that divide also serve to help people if not unite, then converge?

Back to our original question: what's the matter? What's the problem? What will we find in this book? Let me provide a brief overview of the three chapters and then wish you a provocative reading experience.

"Faith of Our Fathers and Mothers" by Jean Bethke Elshtain

Whom does Jean Bethke Elshtain represent, and why was she asked to be part of the team of co-authors? I know from longer conversations through the years with her as my colleague at the University of Chicago that she hovers, as she once put it, "between Wittenberg and Rome," where I place myself, though less hoveringly, with one foot planted in Wittenberg's Lutheranism. She was selected as part of this team of authors as a preeminent political scientist/theologian and for expertise associated with that.

Philosopher George Santayana spoke of religions as representing "worlds" or "rooms." The walls do not all break down, and the religions do not merge. The story behind each has its own particularities and idiosyncrasies. And the power of these faiths and their communities issues precisely from those peculiar features of their stories. It is not necessary, urged Santayana, for anyone who comes upon these worlds or rooms to accept and approve all of what goes on there. That would be impossible to do, because there is often such disparity and contradiction among them. But at the very least one should recognize where one finds oneself, what goes on there, and the like.

Walk into Elshtain's room then, seeing it as a kind of mental furnished apartment, a hospitable place for taking up unfamiliar subjects.

Like right off, page one, "God talk" and "rights talk." She may take for granted that these are the ways Americans speak, and she may well be right about that. But they do not do so customarily and readily in the same chamber. Religion—s-h-h-h! one hears—is a private affair. Keep it restricted to sanctuaries and homes, chapels and retreat centers. Don't blurt in what we might call "religionese" in public unless you are ready to confuse some, embarrass others, antagonize not a few, and slow things down in general. No, Elshtain has overheard and listened for the ways Americans really do speak. She has heard politicians during campaigns, watched rallies for civil rights, noted the garb of demonstrators and the outreach of pulpiteers. Conclusion: "God talk," and what it signifies, is all over the place.

Just as stupefying or bemusing as God talk in the politics chamber is political talk in the religion chamber—both talks welcomed and heard in Elshtain's single room, according to her chapter. Here again the uninitiated or those preoccupied with other concerns may not be quite ready for what they will read. Christ and Caesar did not get along well. The Dalai Lama is acceptable as a religious sage, but one does not have to be very subtle to notice that the Chinese government does not want him to have any bearing on the politics of Tibet. Preachers are urged to deal with things of soul and spirit. But let them touch on housing and poverty, atomic weaponry, or planned parenthood, and you will see half their congregations disappear. But not if Professor Elshtain has anything to do about it. She hears the two kinds of talk going on and pleads for our patience by plunging right ahead.

While today Americans recognize their pluralism and know that suppressed diversity always marked our spiritual landscape, over the last half millennium certain languages became privileged or held dominance. Not Spanish, Portuguese, or French Catholic language, though it came to dominate much of the hemisphere, and certainly not the Native American discourse on the sacred and how people should arrange their lives together. The pioneers and early winners were European Protestants. But they mingled their speech with that of the Enlightenment—a philosophy of reason to some and a new eighteenth-century religion, "Enlightenment with a capital 'E' " to historian Crane Brinton—and left their stamp on the political culture.

The two came together with other voices to produce a new unfolding: religious liberty. It had been hinted at before, but American constitutionalists worked to effect it, and citizens have been busy working it out ever since. Get Americans together to talk "God talk" and "rights talk" in the same room, and you will find that all—or almost all—sides give mantra treatment to the words "free exercise" and "no establishment" of religion. The sixteen words of the First Amendment to the Constitution take on an almost sacred character and offer the best hope for starting and advancing serious debate and free governmental life.

Many authors would go on, have gone on, and are going on, to bewail the presence of the two talkings in one room. Some who would call themselves secularists on one hand, or advocates of private religion on the other, would bemoan the fact that God talk is violating the terms of co-existence and polluting the atmosphere in this setting. Many who would be called religionists on the other hand complain that nonreligious voices outshout them, that secularist ears ignore them, or at the very least that religions other than theirs have been privileged.

"No whining!" insists Elshtain, who has no time for that. But she does find it valuable to call upon someone else to help provide perspective on her enterprise. We have a guest. Picture a foreign visitor coming in, walking around, being attentive, taking notes, and then offering comment. In Elshtain's case it is, unsurprisingly, Alexis de Tocqueville, a French visitor in our past.

Alfred North Whitehead once said that the history of Western philosophy is a series of footnotes to Plato. Elshtain might be ready to remark that the history of the observing of American democracy is a sequence of endnotes to Tocqueville. Her choice of him is not eccentric, nor is he marginal to the enterprise of interpretation. One does not have to associate with hyperbolists to hear, and perhaps to agree, that his classic *Democracy in America* remains the most provocative analysis of our enduring, yet always adjustable, ways.

Little wonder that Tocqueville, heir of a family that survived the

Ancien Regime and the Terror around the French Revolution, would find the American resolution of his day remarkable. And Elshtain, now reading him closely, figuratively using him as a guide to today's America, and thus following him around, similarly finds it noteworthy—if precarious. Tocqueville and now Elshtain both converge on the notion of *civil society*. On its terrain and in its public spheres we are supposed to work things out. When we can't, we go to court. And, rues Elshtain, we go to court quite often these days. Civil society is in trouble.

Owners of this book would be well advised to mark, and borrowers to put a temporary stick-um note, where Elshtain introduces civil society, which she defines with precision; it is going to play a big role in this project. Another mark or sticker goes to the words "voluntary association." The earlier Americans had invented the democratic society's version of these; Tocqueville had seen their decisive role in shaping and serving civil society; Elshtain joins him in recognizing how strategic is the role of religion in promoting such association.

As I read Elshtain, I find her following the course of religion in the democracy along a pilgrim's progressive route full of hazards and new opportunities, but always change. To take one instance with which readers will have to reckon: what happens or what has happened as a consequence of the fact that responsibility for religious rights has for sixty years been progressively related to the federal, not state, government, and especially to the courts? This change is at the root of many current debates about religion in public life, for example, in respect to the issue of prayer in public schools.

There is no way to move along the path of a liberal society without having to deal with the issue of tolerance, for tolerance to the point that it seems to encourage indifference to religion is one of its marks. But can attention to toleration also lead to suppression of the religious voice, just because it is so often abrasive?

Elshtain the political philosopher and theologian at the same time is also always the teacher. While no one is likely to complain that she will not have packed enough substance, lecture-style, into her chapter, everyone will see her doing what good teachers do: she leaves us with projects, questions, and models for pursuing them.

"Standing at the Precipice:
Faith in the Age of Science and Reason"
by Azizah Y. al-Hibri

Whom does Azizah Y. al-Hibri represent, and why was she asked to be one of the co-authors of this book? In planning this work the advance committee was not trying to be representative along the old lines of "equal time" or other discredited theories that used to mark religious studies at universities. That is, people were *not* to be representatives of their communions, if they have them. I know from long conversations that Professor al-Hibri is a committed Muslim—and a committed feminist law professor. Whoever thinks that the Muslim community took a vote and said "this is our spokesperson" does not know that community. Let me also add, however, that there are no reasons for its leaders to suspect that al-Hibri will deviate from devotion to the Qur'an, which she knows better than many who would criticize her. What she does here is not represent Islam so much as the voice of "the other," the often excluded, those who might bring a fresh perspective for analyzing existing worldviews, as she does.

In the culture of the recent past, where what used to be called "political correctness" dominated, we might still have heard sneers about the dominance of dead white European males in the discourse about civil society. Even where such abrupt and ideological dismissals would have no place, the enduring culture of America is rich with other voices from other rooms, all of them ready now to speak, and al-Hibri provides such a voice.

Sometimes when people familiar with the accounting of Puritan Protestant, British Enlightenment, and liberal roots hear these other voices, they may seem jarring, unsettling, and at their worst rooted in myths and mythologies that are hard to connect with the inherited story.

Thus when the Native American hears celebrations of the Constitution and its First Amendment assuring religious freedom, the voices will sound foreign. The Constitution had no room for Indians except as a foreign power, and most religious people of European heritage had no term for them other than "savages." Not until

well into the twentieth century did they come into the scope of constitutional protection. Just before the end of the same century they
still found that many of their assumptions about the sacred, con-
nected with landscapes, or the sacrament, in the form of forbidden
substances, were not given the protection that many other religious
expressions were assured. When they tell the American story, it is
vastly different from the account of the liberal tradition.

When African-Americans hear the same liberal story, they also
listen as if from a room down the hall, with different hearings and
languages. Their ancestors were officially only three-fifths of a
human being when the Constitution was drafted. Most of them
were enslaved until 1863, and the vast majority of them were not
assured taken for granted civil rights until 1965. What has this liberal tradition done for them lately?

To the Protestants, other Christians, and Jews, a Martin Luther
King could in effect say, "85% of the citizens claim to be moved
and judged by Isaiah and Jesus, inspired by visions of a Promised
Land and a new Kingdom. If so, I insist that you act upon your texts
and beliefs." And he could pull the Declaration and Constitution
out of his pocket and treat them as virtual sacred documents of the
civil tradition, and say to the 100 percent that makes up the citizenry,
"I insist. . . ." that you include us in the scope of protection.

In the meantime, this African-American tradition could demonstrate that few religious traditions had better exemplified life in the
Tocquevillean world of voluntary associations than had they.
Whether in slave or segregated society, they never had the luxury
of being pure individualists, even had they chosen to call that a luxury. And they were not in position to be regarded with much dignity by the federal government until the New Deal in the 1930s,
through the World War in the 1940s, or during the civil rights movement of the 1950s and 1960s. Nor could they pull strings in the phil-
anthropic world, though they did not go wholly unnoticed by it.

Instead they had to take care of their own, and did so through
local congregations, self-help agencies, and other associations that
would have pleased Tocqueville. Indeed, at the turn of the century
W.E.B. DuBois, on his way out of church into eventual Marxist
atheism, could still speak of one of the denominations as the finest
invention of black Americans. To this day, when predominantly

black areas experience sudden destruction, it is the churches that are first and alone on the scene to rebuild.

To the Native American and African-American cultures and voices one could add those of the Hispanic, Latino-Latina Americans, who bring their stories, suspicions, and hopes not on the east-west passage but on the south-north nexus and route. The rest of America is just beginning to hear their accounting of the problems and promise of civil society as now constituted. Whether one is listening to a wealthy, politically conservative Miami Cuban; a poor, politically liberal Mexican migrant who has just won citizenship; a New York Puerto Rican airlifted to Spanish Harlem, all of them members of vital subcommunities, there will be considerable differences among their stories and between theirs and what Elshtain calls "the traditional" one.

Lest this catalog grow too long, let me only mention that our country also has a heritage that includes Chinese, Japanese, and Korean Americans, and since changes in the immigration laws in 1965, the voices from rooms populated by Asians also include large numbers of "boat people," Vietnamese, Cambodians, Laotians, Hmong, and more. They all have their retellings to voice. For many these are stories of discrimination and the grudging acceptance of the neighbors. For others these are stories of rapid climb up the success ladder and positive positioning in the land of the free. But they do not come from where Locke and Rousseau, Tocqueville and Madison have spoken.

Enrich all these samplings with religion stories and one can only imagine how diverse the accounting would be. Not that Protestants, Catholics, Jews, Muslims, Baha'is and the others who account for the more than 200 separate denominations in the yearbooks, or the 1,200 religious movements in the encyclopedias, do not have anything in common. The relative functioning of this democracy and its institutions; the common experiences of surviving depressions and wars; the common grieving over assassinations and disasters and common celebration of victories from the Olympics to the battlefield; the better results of common schooling: all these contribute to some common language and concern. But what Santayana called the particularities and idiosyncracies give life to them in their differences.

Merely to provide a guidebook to the different rooms in the American civil house, to take a roll call of all those on pilgrimage toward a civil society, is not very helpful. We do better to take a stop along the way, to listen to the witness of someone who speaks out of—no one "represents"—a distinctive, large, growing, and rich in potential community. Azizah al-Hibri knows Islam well, is devoted to it, brings her own voice of dissent (as a Muslim feminist), is academically and professionally well poised as a professor of law, and has a global perspective as a visitor to Muslim communities worldwide and on the boundaries among Muslims, Jews, Christians, secularists, and more. No one asked all of the varieties to agree on her as their spokesperson. The American Assembly asked Professor al-Hibri to speak.

What I called earlier the "myth" that is part of the stories in civil society will show up on her pages. By myth, scholars of religion are not judging the truth or falsehood of a proposition or a tale. They instead refer to the fact that peoples have ways of expressing themselves in certain stories and frameworks that are not arbitrary; indeed, the point cannot be made in any other way. Thus the Qur'anic myth differs from the Hebrew or Christian scriptural myth, from Hindu or Enlightenment myths. Reading Professor al-Hibri, then, is an exercise in being schooled by an experienced teacher who shares much, very much, with an Elshtain, but also brings difference.

The myth that al-Hibri visits, examines, and chooses to de-mythologize—pardon the term imported from theologians—has to do with what she calls the "mechanistic model of the Industrial Revolution." If Elshtain has one accounting for the fact that religious voices had long been muffled from the political conversation in a religiously rich society, al-Hibri is going to take the reader into a room whose view is obscured in part by a worldview that reduces religious concerns so that they will fit into or be displaced by assumptions that go with this mechanistic model.

Certainly, that is a different story. It will evoke all kinds of protesting or cautioning voices by experts in the hermeneutics of suspicion. It will spell civic hope for some and look like a distortion to others. In that sense, it will provoke responses similar to those that will greet Elshtain's liberal review and vision. But they will come from a different but no less assured citizen.

Through the past two centuries since the Industrial Revolution and the technological successors to it, all kinds of religious voices have protested what Professor al-Hibri calls "dehumanization, fragmentation, and conflict." One hears them speaking up when medical care turns too specialized and uncaring. It comes in response to protest against the bureaucratization of life, with the impersonalization that follows. Put an "-ation" at the end of a word that once described a process, and you come close to talking about the professor's "mechanistic" model.

If such protest and caution sound familiar, al-Hibri's distinctive contribution is to apply it to the rigidities of boundary that have come to mark American life, particularly in its legal forms. Very specifically, "the endless debate over the separation of church and state" reflects the mechanistic model applied to religion and law, in her view.

If Elshtain ends with civil hope, be ready to find al-Hibri starting with it. Early on she will be challenging the obsolete but still oppressive mechanistic model with the dynamics of the Age of Information, which has the potential of being relational, having more room for expressions of personhood. Her argument will surprise some who have seen the Age of Information, the Internet, cyberspace, as accelerations, rapidations—I borrow that word from a Dutch priest—of mechanistic forces. But hear al-Hibri out and you will see how and why she sees hope for it, for religious minorities, for civil society.

So it is that instead of revisiting the British Enlightenment, the thought of the Founding Fathers, and the invention of American institutions, she sets out to explain present discontents and prospects by reference to a mini-history of science and technology. She will also ask for a level playing field, this time for religionists who do not want to be banished from the civil game because they refuse to be mystified by scientific terminology and—relevant to the present theme—"unjustified *secular political authority*."

Those who cherish such authority and see threats to it from vital new religious communities (of ancient stock!) will get their backs up as they read such accusations as those Professor al-Hibri brings. But they had better get used to hearing them, as they come not only from her and her community. If critics do not like it and since they cannot squelch it, they would do better to find strategies of accommodation or rejection.

A voice from her sponsors: if Elshtain can invoke great figures from her political past, now al-Hibri will remind readers of the scientific and technological advances—and they are many—made by Muslims in the past. This is important, since she has to show that this faith is not hostile to science as such. She finds present day company among thinkers who question the hegemony of science, or at least of one of talking about it. Advocates of alternative medicine, alternative to that which follows the "mechanistic model," will also be called in as allies.

If the professor's concerns will first deal with the ways this model of mind undercuts democratic life and stifles invention and innovation in many fields, she is most pressed to show how she thinks it hurts the whole society, its concepts and practices. Here the voice of religion will come in. To make this case she has to challenge mechanistic ways of looking at separation of church and state and, apparently less radically but with profound effect, separation between public and private.

By this point she will come to the specific agenda of this book as a whole: how to deal with common good questions, given the diversity among and disparity of the communities and their voices. Here, as when introducing the Elshtain essay, it is tempting for me to detail her plot and to engage her in argument. But the plot will become clear to readers, and the argument will be more rich and less confusing if she gets to state the issues and terms, as she does.

Finally, she will provide a map of the ways one might conceive church and state. Here they come: *Strict Separationism. The Endorsement Approach. The Accommodationist Approach.* What she sees and warns against in these should, as she expounds it, evoke discussion and prompt approaches by non-Muslims. She chooses to make her way by reference to a very explicit myth, "Adam's Modern Folly," as anticipated in a Biblical/Qur'anic story. (How recently would many have protested the combination implied by the slanting line in that combination! Now it makes its own sense.)

Since we conceive this book as another invitation to civil dialogue, readers have a right to learn some rules of the game, to get some coaching and encouragement to play. Conveniently for us and them, Professor al-Hibri very neatly sets forth ten "proposals" and spells them out with sufficient clarity that they can be put to work.

"From Battleground to Common Ground: Religion in the Public Square of 21st Century America" by Charles C. Haynes

Having commented on the personal perspectives of the other two authors, I should be consistent and provide some insight about Charles C. Haynes; however, I have not the faintest idea where if anywhere he hangs a denominational hat, whom he represents, and who would be put off if they thought Charles was supposed to be representing them. The planners selected him because they discerned that public education and policies having to do with the post-welfare society are among the most hotly contested and most promising, and he is expert in them. They wanted a case study, and he is a veteran with an institutional or associational base who can supply that out of personal experience, as the other three of us in this book cannot.

Both professors' chapters end with a word of hope. Jean Bethke Elshtain advocates a "critical-hopeful" model for nurturing a civil society and "for the common good." Azizah al-Hibri advances proposals that she "hopes" would bring about a form of that common good that had room for "cooperation, neighborliness, and robust faith."

In harmony with both of his colleagues, Charles C. Haynes speaks in a hopeful, faith-full spirit, offering a compelling concluding chapter. His title is tantalizing. "From Battleground to Common Ground." Does that mean he can report that the move has been made, that the ground has shifted under our feet and before our eyes, and that "common ground" and "common good" are in range? Or does it mean that they are out of range, off on a distant horizon but still in reach, and that Haynes describes and offers proposals that will help effect the common goal? Either question is promising, and we, as readers, shall observe him pursuing answers to them.

The book was designed, in part, to illustrate that innovative things are being tried. It offers not only to undertake a historical review and offer models that, in the eyes of some, could sound abstract, but also to provide real-world examples. Nor do we only offer critiques of the turns modern "mechanistic" society has taken and let things go with broad brush strokes as our residue. (Both Professors Elshtain and al-Hibri are known for being "practical" philosophers, theologians, in love with the concrete *polis*, the human city, never content to take refuge in abstract ideals that find no embodiment.)

Instead, it was important to have a case study, a story, a close-up of the way some thoughtful people have set out to experiment with notions having to do with the common good and to pursue strategies that advance them. The natural person to whom to turn was Dr. Haynes, and the staging ground for the case, also naturally, was the field of education, particularly of schooling. We gave him license and encouragement to tell a personal story that has far more than personal implications and does not represent advertising of a particular curricular framework.

In fact, Haynes is only part of a larger movement, though he is large in it. This movement is in the hands of people who are not content to leave the American scene in disarray or divided by warring parties in battle array. One hears much about "culture-wars" at the turn of the millennium, wars to which James Davison Hunter has given the name. There is no doubt that they are going on. Anyone knows this who listens to talk radio, attends a PTA meeting while a school district fights over school prayer, sits in on a religious denominational convention torn apart by debates over homosexuality, overhears "family values" arguments, or ducks when missiles fly between pro-choice and pro-life camps disputing abortion policies. Such fights enliven the republic. They are signs of vitality among sub-publics and on selective issues. Whoever believes in republican life has to see such contentions as being preferable to indifference, apathy, or comatoseness.

Well and good. Or not well enough or not good enough. In any case, the figuratively armed camps in such conflicts by no means represent most citizens or all options. They may passionately believe that they do pursue the common good, and no historian who has observed battles over slavery, women's rights, or civil rights is going to minimize the contributions of those who bring firm conviction, ambition, staying power, and emotion to their causes. But many among them can also find themselves seeking the self-interest of their cause and their group and leaving the majority alienated or moved to fall into silence.

As I read the battleground story in Haynes's chapter, there came to mind once again an image that talk of culture-wars often leaves. Picture two mesas, high above a plain. Imagine atop these two high tablelands are the instruments of war, artillery, pointed at the other side. Conceive of them firing away, lobbing great shells, and sometimes even sending forth lethal gases. They are minorities. On almost all vital issues dividing the republic you will find that 5 to 15 percent are wholly convicted activists. Add the two and you have from 70 to 90 percent of the people less motivated, more confused about their beliefs, less committed to one or the other side of the dividing causes, dwelling on the plain between the two mesas.

These citizens know that they are in the valley of decision, but rarely do their decisions match those represented by the polarities for clarity or in their extremity. They live with some ambiguity, some contradiction; they know that not everything at issue will be satisfied in their lifetime or to their satisfaction. They will often change their place on the plain as they try to keep distance from the side that has fired most recently. They find hollows and gulches into which they can duck for refuge when the shells, bullets, and gases get too close to them. Now and then a few will climb a mesa and be converted to a side.

Whatever else happens on this landscape, it is not a signal that the search for the common good, the common ground is prime. To speak of such common ground, in the worlds of Elshtain, al-Hibri, and now Haynes, is emphatically not to pursue settlement with middling positions, mediocrities, or wishy-washy resolutions. Instead, as the Haynes case shows, the most farseeing and daring of them venture with new strategies, new tactics, new ways to frame questions.

As these two parties lob missiles and point their weapons at each other or anyone who steps into the no-person's land between them, some courageous souls step forward. They advocate positions that may not please either the privilegers of specific, e.g., Christian, faith on one hand or those who want to keep religion off the school premises on the other. But they do find approaches that are constitutional, educationally sound, fair in their treatment of the situation in pluralist America, and thus potential contributors to the common good.

When they get together, their company on the figurative plain often leads to the formation of strange alliances. When civil liberty groups like People for the American Way and the American Jewish Congress on one side link with some evangelical Protestant groups such as the Christian Legal Society and the National Association of Evangelicals, many old warriors would have to rub their eyes. But read Haynes and see in print the assertion that they did line up together on this issue. In fact, in a second run at listing them he adds more groups that one would not expect to see listed on the same side on the same page.

The consensus report of this Assembly, whether or not it always uses the term, proposes teaching "about" religion, a somewhat clumsy and never fully accurate approach, but we will live with its shortcomings rather than cater to the extremes and fall into unconstitutional positions on one side or miseducational ones on the other.

Is it too much to suggest that such citizen endeavors have "trickle-up" effects? During the years when these momentary, practical, and tentative alliances were forming, the president of the United States in 1999 defined national policies on the subject of teaching about religion in public schools. Remarkably, bitter foes of that president ceased fire and often quoted his statements, seeing them to be constructive. Meanwhile old-time "secularist" enemies of religion in public places at least grudgingly—but often with measured enthusiasm—recognized the potential of better, more realistic, education occurring. And all sides had to see the congruence such approaches had with the United States Constitution and Supreme Court decisions that prohibited school prayer but encourage "teaching about. . . ."

The observation of such culture-warring and fresh strategic experiment frames the chapter and program of Charles C. Haynes. He begins by reference to the Williamsburg Charter, a pioneering

(1988) attempt to find alternatives to culture-wars. That charter was based in updated and reinterpreting approaches to the First Amendment, which so often becomes the structure behind "common ground" talk. So devoted are many to that base that the First Amendment's sixteen words concerning religion could be chipped into marble or bronzed and would then serve as an icon, a shrine, a sacred object.

Haynes will take the Williamsburg Charter and "a number of recent civic initiatives—many involving public education" as signs of hope. His chapter will deal chiefly with the second of these, public education, his own field of expertise. His historical review of failed experiments points to what have become dead-end alleys down which a loud minority still seeks to go. But they cannot be stifled or outflanked if they are met only by naysayers. In the Haynes chapter we shall see what forms of yeasaying have the most positive effect and how these proposals have met constitutional tests.

Perhaps I have overstressed the curricular, the substantive "content-wise" dimensions of such work. Haynes immediately moves on to show how other aspects of the religion-in-education enterprise look in the light of consensus reached so far. These have to do with calendars, religious holidays, garb, equal access to school space in before- or after-school programs. None of them is a cause or issue that will ever be addressed to the full satisfaction of all parties. But their "civic agreement" does result from a process manifestly superior to the "culture-wars" approach and, Haynes will argue, shows promise for future development on other unfinished and, shall we suggest, never-to-be finished civil and educational business.

Whether or not readers will buy into the "Three R's" project ("rights, responsibilities, and respect") they will, as a result of reading Haynes's chapter, have at least become acquainted with one of the models or paradigms for which Elshtain and al-Hibri have asked.

"If so much potential is there, why have I not heard about it?" you may be wondering. That's a legitimate question for many school superintendents (all of whom have had a chance to read about it, if they read their mail containing comprehensive guidelines on religion sent at the direction of President Clinton by the U.S. Department of Education to every public school in the nation), teachers, parents, and civic-minded people. Haynes has to take up that question and at least implicitly invite readers who share his pre-suppositions to speak up and advocate such programs. Some of the foot dragging on the part of those who do know of the possibilities occurs because of legal uncertainties; these make school adminis-trators wary. I am happy to say that Haynes does not minimize the legal complexities, and he takes issue with some decisions already made.

His main argument is with public school educators who have failed to capture this vision. He does not pursue it from a mesa whence he can lob bombs and where he can put up barricades against the artillery of the educators. Nor are they arrayed in an armed camp. Much philosophical debate and many alertings of the value of the new educational approaches within a pluralist so-ciety are in the offing.

To no one's surprise, Haynes recognizes that "teaching about" religion in respect to public issues such as homosexuality and abor-tion will be most difficult, and he tells why—and why it is of value to deal with them respectfully.

Not all efforts to pursue common ground affect public schools. There are other initiatives, such as "charitable choice" (i.e., the pro-vision of the 1996 welfare reform legislation that specifies that state governments cannot discriminate against religious groups when contracting for services to help move welfare recipients into the workforce, nor can they require such groups to give up their reli-gious values when acting as social service providers) that are promis-ing to some, threatening to others, and at least broached by Haynes. He details them, so I need not.

Joining Professor al-Hibri in acting on an educator's impulse, he proposes nine steps to match her ten. We are, again, on the soil of a practitioner who knows the lay of the land. If he does not end with words about hope, he has pointed to people and projects that embody such hope. And if, with late theologian and philoso-pher Father John Courtney Murray, Haynes does not think we will come to "articles of faith" in and about the republic, he thinks with Murray again that we can find and live by some "articles of peace." And thus move toward common ground for the common good.

A Final Note

To bring in-house clarity to the origins of this book and the Assembly on religion in American public life, I turn to those who "provided the great big room," "invited in all kinds of people," and got them talking. They are Daniel A. Sharp, president and CEO of The American Assembly, and Debra Burns Melican, who directs the *Uniting America* series of which this is a part. While they cajoled me into taking the chairmanship of this venture and helping edit this book and have uttered their thanks for my doing so, I want to turn this around now and say thanks to them for the challenge and the opportunity. I have learned much already from the people they brought together, the readings, and the process that The American Assembly has devised—concluding after this exercise, "it works." If anything they say in describing the book and the series program revisits some of the themes I have addressed there, I believe readers will find that they contribute to clarity about some hard to define issues, and will help advance the conversation that we hope will issue from this and the other four books growing out of the *Uniting America* series. My thanks to all who made this project possible, and especially to the co-directors and co-authors, Jean Bethke Elshtain, Azizah Y. al-Hibri, and Charles C. Haynes.

Now, let us turn to the heart of this book and think more about why faith matters, the story of religion in American public life.

1

Faith of Our Fathers and Mothers: Religious Belief and American Democracy

Jean Bethke Elshtain

"God talk" at least as much as "rights talk" is the way Americans speak. American politics is indecipherable if severed from the panoply and interplay of America's religions, most importantly Protestantism derived from various offshoots of Calvinism and Methodism. Much of our political ferment historically and currently flows from religious commitments. The majority of Americans have long believed that our history of religious liberty—free exercise coupled with disestablishment—is what distinguishes America from so many other polities.[1] Currently some 95 percent of Americans claim belief in God and fully 70 percent membership in a church, synagogue, or mosque. What this signifies is in need of interpretation, certainly, but our significant embrace of faith as a

JEAN BETHKE ELSHTAIN is Laura Spelman Rockefeller Professor at the University of Chicago Divinity School. Previously she taught at the University of Massachusetts and Vanderbilt University, where she was the first woman to hold an endowed professorship in the history of that institution. She has been a visiting professor at Oberlin College, Yale University, and Harvard University. Dr. Elshtain is the recipient of four honorary degrees and is a fellow of The American Academy of Arts and Sciences.

grounding of human meaning, purpose, and identity and as a distinguishing feature of our culture also builds a variety of tensions and conflicts into the very tissue of American life. Perhaps a summary conceptual and historic backdrop will help us to appreciate a characteristic of America that continues to bewilder foreign visitors to our shores as much as it transfixed the famous Frenchman, Alexis de Tocqueville, whose work on our democracy helped to capture the tone and temperament of the fledgling republic over a century and a half ago.

The American constitutional republic was forged in and through a complex intermingling of religious and political imperatives, from the Puritans' famous "city on a hill" up to present debates and events. Although church and state are kept separate—ours is neither a theocracy nor a nation with an *official* civic religion—religion and politics have always mutually constituted one another in ways direct and indirect. As political theorist George Armstrong Kelly noted a quarter of a century ago:

> Although it is less evident today than it was fifty years ago, a great deal of the American ethos—in politics as well as in manners and morals—was created by a complex interweaving of Puritan Calvinism and Methodist Arminianism. The balancing action of the one in the sphere of faith and the other in public affairs underlay the "harmonization" theme of Tocqueville's theory.[2]

Kelly here refers to a theme advanced by Alexis de Tocqueville in his masterwork, *Democracy in America,* where Tocqueville proclaimed that the religiously formed and shaped democratic optimism and the associational enthusiasm he saw all around him when he toured these United States during the Jacksonian era were something new under the political sun. To Tocqueville, this represented nothing less than a "harmonization of heaven and earth." To speak of this robust interplay of religion and politics is to put into play conceptually and practically a number of important categories, including believer and citizen, church and state. The terrain in which they meet, most of the time, is that realm of institutional and associational life called *civil society.* From time to time—these moments should be rare, although, alas, they seem to be more frequent all the time—the meeting ground will be the courts. But if the courtroom is the venue, it suggests that the delicate *modus vivendi* worked

out all over America in thousands of differently structured and populated communities has, at least for that moment, broken down.
How so?

Let's begin with the notion of civil society. To speak of civil society is to speak of culture generally, of the institutions that human
beings create for themselves in order to raise their children, sustain
work life, strive to prosper, guarantee domestic peace and safety,
propagate their faith, enact projects of solidaristic purpose, and attain individual ends and purposes. Looking at American culture
over its historic span, we see straight away that the distinctive culture of English Puritan dissenters transported to our shores, one that
embodied a faith fully integrated into culture, lost ground rather
quickly. But the legacy lingers. A great strength of Puritan religion
was its institutional anchoring in the covenantal tradition. The local
congregation embodied the Kingdom of God in America, and
America herself was a New Jerusalem. There was a distinctly mil-
lennialist flavor to the enterprise. Although Puritanism faded,
Protestant hegemony of American religious life remained, sustained
through what has been called the "semi-establishment" of Protestant Christianity as a civic religion, pervasive if unofficial. The Bible
read in common schools, once they were created, was the King
James version. School prayers might include the Lord's Prayer as
well as a combination of patriotic and devotional supplications. It
was this dimension of American religion that most caught
Tocqueville's attention. But his discerning eye and ear also placed
within the American dispensation a community of faith that many
in nineteenth century America held to be incompatible with American democracy, namely, Roman Catholicism.

Tocqueville on Religion, Democracy, and Habits of the Heart

By the time Tocqueville toured America (c. 1830) much had already changed. The nation's purpose had spread and now embodied something like manifest destiny—looking westward—even as the
older Puritan establishment had lost its hold. The congregation had
somewhat weakened or altered as well, coming to be construed
rather more along the lines of a voluntary association or social con-

tract than a powerful and binding covenant between God and His people. Catholicism was an exception, as was Judaism, but it remained the case that the majority of Americans were religious seekers and believers of a Protestant variety who saw in communal liberty the freedom to *be* religious rather than freedom *from* religion. The United States Constitution, unlike, say, the terms under which Jewish residents of the nation were incorporated into the polity in France, had not required, as the price of civic admission, that Jews give up the communal dimensions of their faith that found expression in and through Hebrew schools, communally enforced dietary rules and regulations and dress, and the like. *Confessional pluralism* and *social pluralism* got linked together in America. The first refers to what is usually called "freedom of conscience"; the latter, to "the maintenance and accommodation of a plurality of associations to foster religion."[3] Tocqueville was less interested in legalities, as we all know, than in what he called the *mores,* the "habits of the heart" that really determine what makes a culture tick. Here social pluralism was most critical as this refers to the sphere we call civic society— the realm of families, schools, learned and civic associations, the variety of plural associations that help people to nurture and to sustain "morality, charity, and discipline in the state and broader community."[4] A humanist and rationalist of sorts, Tocqueville wasn't particularly sympathetic to the extraordinary energies of American evangelism—his reaction being: "From time to time strange sects arise which endeavor to strike out extraordinary paths to eternal happiness. Religious insanity is very common in the United States"—but he did see how thoroughly religion and politics were saturated with one another and in ways that he found not incidental to American political culture but as forming its very core.

Tocqueville, a French Catholic whose family narrowly escaped complete devastation during the Terror, understood what happened when a people's religion is violently wrenched from them. This "enervates" and depletes a culture; it does not liberate. So Tocqueville's discerning eye was shaped by the memories of direct experiences. But he also knew that the long story of Western encounters between *regnum,* or earthly rule, and *sacerdotium,* or the sacred and its representation on earth, is rich and complex—much more than simply a matter of "state" hostility to "church." The West had never been

deeply receptive to a thoroughgoing theocratic model in which political and religious establishments are fused into a monistic structure. There were often close alliances between throne and altar in
Western Christendom, to be sure, but this isn't the same thing. A
differentiation between politics and religion was sown in Western
religious history from very early on, quite pointedly so with the
coming of Christianity. Christians were obliged to ask: what has
Christ to do with Caesar? The answer varied widely—and still does.

Let's add to this mix the fact that the church, the synagogue before it and ongoingly, to which must now be added the mosque in
light of the growing number of Muslim Americans, embodied and
embody a kind of alternative politics. Each faith tradition has its
own understanding of community membership, authority, rule,
power, and the nature of earthly kingdoms in general.[5] The
postmedieval history of the West is a story of the various comings
together and subsequent teasing apart of church and state. But religion and politics are something else, as already noted. Tocqueville,
then, simply took account of what Americans have always believed,
namely, that these cannot be separated as too much of the same ter-
ritory is claimed by each. Consider the American experiment with
this claim in mind. We begin—if one traces the foundations of con-
stitutionalism rather than of early Puritan establishment—with no
establishment of religion but with the free exercise of religion. Responsibility for protecting religious rights and liberties lay almost entirely with the states for at least 150 years.[6] What were the
implications of this radical idea? Bear in mind at this point that the
views of a few of the great Founders of this republic were somewhat anomalous, Jefferson among them who famously proclaimed
that it mattered not whether his neighbor believed in no God or
twenty gods: it neither picked his pocket nor broke his leg. The vast
majority of Americans, at least historically, have not been so indif-
ferent about their neighbor's beliefs. One might say that Jefferson
himself was a member of a religious minority as a rationalist and
deist of sorts. His countrymen and women, however, mingled in all
sorts of ways their everyday activities in work and home and community and their Sunday professions of faith in church.

It is utterly unsurprising, then, that when Tocqueville toured
America in the Jacksonian era he wrote of the ways in which reli-

gion in the United States, by which he meant Christianity in its various incarnations, including Catholicism, generated and made use of democratic instincts: religion helped to shape the mores, the habits of the heart, in his famous phrase. Tocqueville further observed that settled beliefs "about God and human nature are indispensable to men for the conduct of daily life"—you simply couldn't function if you awakened each morning and had to determine what truths would guide you over the next twenty-four hours.[7] So for any culture the question will be: what forms the basis of the truths that guide us? The truths that set the *mores* for Americans were, in one way or another (with but few exceptions) theistically grounded. So much so that Tocqueville insisted that America embodied a coming age of democracy and equality, not despite her religiosity but precisely *because* of it.

How so? Because one could not understand the great movement toward equality without understanding the Christian insistence that all are equal in the eyes of God. This equality, enacted politically, brings great benefits. Tocqueville was visiting us just as what came to be known as nineteenth century religious optimism was about to take off. This optimism about human beings and God got ingrained early in the century as the strict Calvinist dispensation waned. American egalitarianism was part and parcel of an optimism about human prospects in general, American prospects in particular.

Few, therefore, wanted to grapple with Tocqueville's musings about the problematic tendencies that an overly optimistic, "can-do," religiously grounded but secular egalitarianism might trail in its wake. Here, in a nutshell, are the worries. Egalitarianism in a commercial republic such as the United States unleashes a materialistic quest. At this juncture, faith communities, not simply as a goad and a kind of adjunct feature of the civic but, rather, in their robust specificity and particularity, are vital. Why? Because such traditions and communal institutions serve as a chastening influence on striving ambition by inspiring contrary urges that draw people into community and away from narrow materialism. Religion, in Tocqueville's words, helps to "purify, control, and restrain that excessive and exclusive taste for well-being human beings acquire in an age of equality."[8] Tocqueville surely had in his sights the early covenantal tradition and its living remnants. The notion of covenant is one that stresses mutual accountability of persons to one another and before God. This creates and sustains "a kind of moral equality among the people," and in this effort, Catholicism plays a central role, too, Tocqueville avers.[9]

His argument goes like this: though American Christians were divided into many sects, their religion in general shapes the mores that help to hold in balance individual liberty and community—at least in an ideal scheme of things. Around 1830 there were about a million Christians professing Catholicism, the majority from Ireland. Tocqueville, going very much against the grain, proclaimed American Catholics "the most republican and democratic of all classes in the United States."[10] How so? Because the sacramental, liturgical, and communal structure of Catholicism emphasizes the equality of all believers on the intellectual level. As well, because most Catholics (at that time) were poor, the stress on opposition to oppression and demands for justice as part of a communal undertaking helped to curb the countervailing tendencies in American culture toward individualism (bad egoism, for Tocqueville) and isolation.

Surprisingly, then, and in sum, the separation of church and state in America invited an astonishingly religious atmosphere in light of our mores. By diminishing the official power of religion, Americans appeared to have enhanced its social strength. Perhaps, deep down, Americans understood that religion feeds hope and is thus attached to a constitutive principle of human nature. Amidst the flux and tumult of rambunctious democratic politics and a commercial republic, religion shaped and mediated the passions. Tocqueville's fear was that were the day to come when those passions got unleashed upon the world unrestrained, then we would arrive at an unhappy moment indeed, a dreary world he called "democratic despotism." This world might eventuate should the claim take hold that each individual is somehow his or her own principle of justification. Such individualistic proclamations of self-sovereignty cannot sustain community and, sadly, will surely undermine over time the deep philosophical and metaphysical principle that all persons are unique and sacred. Here it is important to underscore Tocqueville's opposition to civil religion. For a *civil* religion, assimilated as such religions are to the state and dominated by considerations of *raison e'etat,* erodes faith over time. Religion turns into pious sentiments and too frequently gets conflated to nationalism. But a republican government such as our own depends on communal vitality and a source of value and purpose not reducible to any single constitution or regime, no matter how well ordered and decent.

Would American religion always remain strong enough to exert a complex role that was simultaneously chastening and invigorating? Here Tocqueville wasn't at all confident about our prospects. He determined that there were at least two great dangers threatening religion and, indirectly, American democracy, namely, *schism* and *indifference.* Schism pits us against one another in suspicion and enmity. Thus American believers seemed determinedly driven to nigh infinite mitosis, Tocqueville noted. If you didn't like the preacher, throw him out. If you can't throw him out, leave that church and start a new one. If there is a credal difference and it sticks in your craw, change it or drop it, and if others don't accept it, start a new church. Small wonder that President Andrew Jackson is supposed to have quipped that political attacks didn't bother him half so much as arguments in the Presbyterian church. If communities are not strong enough to hold together, individuals will not only fly away, they may fly apart. Note that this tendency feeds directly into our present dilemmas about difference. If and when our differences become destructive divisions, that is schism: we fly apart and can find no judicious principle of comity. This erodes our appreciation of both community and plurality as we need communities in order to make our differences manifest and present to one another in a nonviolent way. But with the breakup of the convenantal tradition, Protestant individualism, by the end of the nineteenth century, held sway to an extraordinary extent. Tocqueville had put his finger on our pulse all right. As covenant increasingly gave way to contract, the range of public debate and discussion also altered. Over time, we felt a good bit more comfortable talking about *interests* than we did talking about *norms* or *principles* or *moral good or goods.* We confidently proclaimed our *rights* but it got to seem excessively dour to discuss our *duties.*

What about the issue of indifference? Indifference is a danger because this attitude invites us not to care about one another at all.

We become *so* latitudinarian we cease to care. In the current lingo: "whatever." This is different from authentic tolerance of the sort that presupposes a way to live together with strong, open, and articulated differences that go deep and are far more than cosmetic. Surely if Tocqueville were in our midst today, he would point to both worries and suggest that we are in a clear and present danger of losing that generous concern for others that religion as institutionally robust faith communities, by contrast to spirituality of the vaporous individualist sort, promotes. Tocqueville would find enormously troubling evidence that suggests Americans are increasingly detached from "religion," or so a recent report suggests in these words: "Where once a community of believers shared a common vocabulary, many feel free to define God by their own lights."[11] That's a lot of lights. The problem, of course, is that purely individualistic lights flicker and go out. A true illumination is provided by people who hold their lights aloft in the darkness as a community of belief. As well, operating from some *common moral basis that does not require doctrinal leveling but does demand searching for certain core norms we share helps people to learn how to compromise because they agree on so many important things.* This agreement does not mean enforced conformity and a unity imposed from above, as will become clearer as we proceed.

Here's the conundrum summarized: if we slide into a world of schism, our differences become occasions for isolation, and we lose authentic pluralism that requires institutional bases from which to operate. It is pluralism that gives us space to be both American and Protestant, Catholic, Jew, Muslim, on and on. Absent robust and vibrant faith and civic institutions, we are thrown back on our own devices; we lose the strength that membership provides; we forget that we can know a good in common that we cannot know alone. Should we arrive at this Tocquevillian impasse, we would find that individuals, striving to stand upright in the winds blowing from centers of governmental or economic power now operating minus that chastening influence from other vital sources, would soon be flattened. People would grow apart and become strangers one to another. We might still have kin, but we would no longer have a country in the strong sense of a polity of which we were essential parts.

The Danger of Dogmatic Skepticism

This is where a form of dogmatic skepticism familiar to us all at present, a skepticism that is corrosive of all faith and all belief save the unexamined belief in skepticism itself, enters. Tocqueville knew that people would always question and challenge. But what happens if there is nothing but skepticism of a dogmatic sort that is unable to sustain any beliefs? Tocqueville would no doubt see Americans at the beginning of the new century in this danger zone as well. Are we, as a culture, undermining our ability to believe and to affirm anything at all save the ephemeral ground of our own subjective experiences? Much current evidence answers in the affirmative, and historians suggest that this reflects the strongly anti-institutional and individualizing tendencies of our culture with its overriding emphasis on personal freedom. No one is opposed to personal freedom. The problem arises when this freedom embraces the poles of either schism or indifference or both, which means, in practice, there are no grounds for nonutilitarian relationships and obligations.

In such a milieu, religion becomes just another voluntary association. You can take it up or drop it if it no longer serves your immediate purposes. But, as democratic defenders and theorists have *known* for centuries, absent strong formative institutions it is impossible to sustain freedom in the authentic sense, freedom of the sort that is necessarily self-limiting because I recognize that *my* freedom is not in opposition to *yours* but that each of us *together* is free insofar as we sustain respect and recognition for others. That, too, is where faith communities play a critical role, for Tocqueville. They must insistently help us to recognize the claims of the "other," the person before us, whatever his or her skin color, ethnicity, economic status, or, yes, religious belief. As Barbara Allen writes in *Tocqueville on Covenant and the American Republic:* "Skepticism, indifference, and relativism encourage habits of thought that ultimately cripple the public arena of debate on which political liberty depends. Rather than freeing our intellectual capacities, disbelief inhibits moral development, threatening the basis for mature political judgment."[12]

Allen continues along these lines: instead of promoting political liberty, disbelief favors secular movements, even factions of an extreme nature. One example would be much current libertarianism of the sort that acknowledges *no* legitimate restraints on individual striving so long as I am not physically harming another—and even that restraint can be got round if we contractually and "freely" agree to harm one another! We say, for example, that much active harm is done to children by excessive representations of violence on television or in video games. But as soon as a public figure, or organized group of citizens, moves to propose ways to limit this violence—even though the means may be voluntary acceptance of "Family Hour" policies for television and the like—libertarian absolutists start to cry "censorship!" This cry stifles citizenship. Over the long run the terrible irony may well be that those who have given themselves over uninhibitedly to a culture of striving and limitlessness will erode our mutual grounding in authentic human rights, which simultaneously free us and constrain us. In our current climate, corrosive features of popular culture and media-driven public opinion, not religious belief, threaten to subvert the mores of self government.

Let's take up the story of how we got to where we are by refracting the conceptual history another way. What follows requires real concentration. Although it is a discussion that is, on some level, familiar to us all, we rarely hold it up to the light for thorough examination. I begin with what I shall call *the liberal paradigm*, for we are a liberal culture through and through by this point. How did we get here?

Religious Belief and the Liberal Paradigm: Conflict, Continuity, and Challenge

It is time to deepen the complexities of the historical and thematic backdrop to this consideration of religion and American public life. If Tocqueville, humanist, Catholic, advocate of republican government, feared the debilitating effects of thoroughgoing skepticism and individualism, there is a cross-cutting tradition that promotes actively skepticism and individualism and does so, its proponents insist, in order to preserve rather than to threaten the status and formation of independent self-governing individuals as citizens of a constitutional order. This is the tradition of philo-

sophical and political liberalism.[13] The standard treatment on liberalism and religion historically is that liberalism forced a regime
of "toleration" on religion. From the point of view of this dominant liberalism, faith communities are paradigmatic examples of
what came to be called "sectarian" groups. The assumption here
taken for granted is that religion always represents a potential menace and might get out of hand if not held in check. Often, even in
current debates, the Spanish Inquisition or some event or incident
of ancient lineage is brought forward as if it were a clear and present danger in early twenty-first century America. But if one looks
at the many instances of persecution of believers, including Christians in many spots on the globe at present, it appears that the
greater danger comes from the side of overweening state power. Yet
religion, more often than not, becomes the bogeyman. How so?

Let's rummage in the pre-liberal past for just a moment in order
to deepen our understanding. Before the emergence of those social
contract theories associated with liberalism, all assumptions about
governance and rule held that government's legitimacy turned on
a divine mandate. This didn't mean a ruler ruled absolutely or
tyrannically. A ruler could violate the office that was his sacred trust,
go from being king to being tyrant, and be openly punished by
tyrannicide. The major point is that rulers were beholden to a
greater power outside themselves for the office they held in trust.
The theory, much transgressed in practice, was that this would stay
the hand of those tempted by excess. All of this was to change.
With the spread of commerce, the breakup of medieval Christendom, the centralization and solidification of monarchies and prin-
cipalities, and, in 1555, the Peace of Augsburg enshrining the *cuius
regio* rule, namely, that the faith of the ruler was the faith of his kingdom, Western Europe moved into a new era. Religious identifica-
tion and being a political subject continued as mutually constitutive.
But a powerful new source of legitimation was located for earthly
rule: it lay with the people, with subjects who had contracted for
that purpose.

Enter the social contract thinkers. The most important to the
American experience is John Locke, associated famously with his
Essay on Toleration (which tolerated all save Catholics, atheists, "id-
iots," etc.) and his classic *Two Treatises of Government*. Locke insisted,

as a precondition for civil government, that religion and government had to be distinguished and lines drawn between them. Locke drew up a strong civic map with religion in one sphere, government in another. A person could be a citizen of each, so long as that citizen never attempted to blend the two. In the religious domain, one answered God's call. But step out of that domain and take one step into the civic realm and God didn't figure directly any more. A citizen's fidelity is pledged to the magistrate. Should the magistracy overstep its bounds, there is always the "appeal to heaven" and the possibility of revolution. But disobedience takes place only in the most extreme situations. Most of the time, religion and government need not meet one another directly. Religion is located as quite irrelevant in a public sense. Note here that, in the words of constitutional scholar Michael McConnell: "Locke's exclusion of atheists and Catholics from toleration cannot be dismissed as a quaint exception to his beneficent liberalism; it follows logically from the ground on which his argument rested. If religious freedom meant nothing more than that religion should be free so long as it is irrelevant to the state, it does not mean very much." Why? Because religion has been privatized and its meaning reduced to the subjective spiritual well-being of each individual religious practitioner.

Madison picked up on certain aspects of Locke; Jefferson, others. But the Lockean formula had finessed as many problems as it had attempted to solve, for human beings cannot, in practice, seal themselves off into compartments and be believers one moment, good subjects of the king the next. Inevitably, the categories bleed into one another. But the "proper spheres" argument persisted, tethered to an optimistic view that religious and governmental jurisdiction would rarely conflict. It is this Lockean liberalism rather than the strong civic republicanism buttressed by civil religion associated with the thinking of Jean-Jacques Rousseau that triumphed in America. Rousseau, in *The Social Contract,* had welded together polity and religion, insisting that no person who was divided in his loyalty and allegiance could be a full-fledged participant in the republic. No one was exempted from the civil religion. Loyalty to the state was the ultimate loyalty that trumps all other forms of fidelity. Rousseau vehemently attacked strong institutional forms of Christianity, like Catholicism, because believers may become conflicted

as to where their allegiances lie. They are placed under a dual obligation. Rousseau described this with contempt as he aimed to break
down any and all strong allegiances save for loyalty to the state.

Though it can be said that America embraced a tacit, "disestablished" civil religion in the dominance of the "Protestant paradigm" of mainline churches, this is a far cry from a Rousseauian
civil religion. It is important to note, however, that this Protestant
civil religion was all too often intolerant historically to other forms
of belief. Indeed, the "common schools" in America were set up
with the explicit task of forming citizens in a single mold and undermining the influence of, or even preventing the development of,
"sectarian" (read parochial) schools. So we have scarcely been exempt from outbursts of intolerance in behalf of a tacit civil religion
that from time to time turned violent: the Know-Nothings, the attacks on Mormons, Jewish quotas, and the like. Nor are we exempt
from an intolerance of the present moment that takes shape as a
deep suspicion of, even contempt for, persons with strong religious
conviction, especially if such persons put those convictions ahead
of loyalty to the state in cases of conflict.[14] Consider, for example,
the general unpopularity of conscientious objectors in time of war.

But let's return to the main story. The final triumph of liberal
philosophical presuppositions in the West is evident in John Stuart
Mill's classic *On Liberty*. Mill is adamantly opposed to civil religion:
that would be an intolerable fusion of power. But he goes on to
express an animus to religion in general. Religion plays to the
"worse" rather than the "better" parts of human nature. Religion
is an activism. Religion is living on borrowed time. One day soon,
in the wake of spreading enlightenment, religion will be overtaken
by an apotheosis of "reason." And reason, for Mill, *must* speak in one
voice. Even as there is a single standard for what is reasonable, religion is by definition ruled out of court as both unreasonable and tolerated only so long as it is privatized. Religion has no place in public
life. Note that if one is looking at these questions from the standpoint
of Mill, the problem is with the nature and character of religion. But
if one refracts the issues differently, it seems that perhaps a shriven
definition of politics is the real problem. How did politics get reduced
almost exclusively to the clash of interests? Can we really not discuss normative claims about human persons and their good in

political life? Keep in mind, then, as we go along that "the problem" we face may, in fact, lie with limitations "in our politics [rather] than from inherent limits in religion."[15] Back to the main story.

How did the victorious Locke-to-Mill liberal paradigm fare on America's shores? How far did the writ of Locke or Rousseau or later Mill run? There are several analytic and historic tracks down which one must move in this matter. Let's call them the "constitutional" and the "popular" or "cultural." The constitutional track is powerfully defined by the First Amendment's protection against establishment and guarantee of free exercise. One could make the case that the astonishing evidence of Americans exercising religions freely, from the inception to the present, turns precisely on nonestablishment. But there are tensions and strains in this picture that draw together the popular and constitutional tracks and help us to account for the fact that so many American citizens who are religious believers are convinced that their society has acted in ways that undermine its commitment to free exercise in a robust sense.

As noted above, for the first 150 years of the republic, primary responsibility for religious rights and liberties was lodged with the states. Attempts to create a national law on religion applicable to the states and enforceable in the federal courts were defeated.[16] This was the norm. But the federal government got into the act in a big way over the last half century. A constitutional position emerged that might be called "strong separationism."[17] Although this position has never held consistent sway, it figures in the thinking of all those, whether in the law or not, who go beyond church-state separation, by seeking a thoroughly secularized society stripped of any and all public markers and reminders of religion. Religion must be privatized and become invisible to public life. There is a built-in animus against the determination by faith communities to sustain their own networks of schools, social provision, civic advocacy groups, health care institutions, and the like, and to see these activities as both religious and civic. In effect, a strong separationist would say, "If you want to be religious you can't be civic, and vice versa," at least as a precondition for receipt of any public monies in support of broad based charitable activities. Strong separationists want to extend the bright line separating church and state to such a line severing religion and politics. This position has never been triumphant in any thoroughgoing way constitutionally speaking, but a number of cases push this direction.

The general drive along the constitutional track has also been marked in liberal political philosophy. It is a position best called *liberal monism*, which holds that all institutions internal to a democratic society must conform to a single authority principle (one person, one vote), a single standard of what counts as reason and deliberation (here Mill and later Millians), and a single vocabulary of political discussion. Reason is defined in such a way that faith is discounted as irrationalism. Christians, Jews, Muslims, any one with faith commitments is not permitted, when speaking *as a citizen,* to give reasons for his or her support or dissent from a public policy measure, say, in language that incorporates any explicit religious reference.[18] Citizens who are also believers are obliged to translate every view supported by their religious beliefs into a civic language of "public reason." Only in this way, claims liberal monism, can America achieve some kind of workable civic consensus. If one refracts these concerns from the standpoint of religious belief, "the problem" looks quite different: what becomes evident is a problem with a narrowing of the purview of politics rather than with religious commitments. Nevertheless, it is religion that is put on the defensive consistently.

Ironically, then, a tradition that emerged in part as a reaction to religious intolerance is now, all too often, intolerant of religion. But the implication of this philosophic stance is often left unexamined, namely, that *American social pluralism,* constituted importantly by the history and presence of diverse faith communities, is undermined and even feared and lamented if we press liberal monism. There are, however, more capacious possibilities that can be derived from the liberal political and philosophical tradition, and these operate informally on the popular level where ordinary citizens are far more tolerant regarding the expression of faith based commitments by their fellow citizens than are many political philosophers and constitutional scholars indebted to a liberal monist paradigm. Still, even on the popular level, there seems to be a drive to privatize religion in part from fear of open challenge and disagreement. If one raises the bar too high—seeking, say, civil harmony and unity rather than the possibility of working and shifting consenses and a comingling of pluralities and commonalities—religious differences are always going to be problematic at best. Religion may even come to be seen as a civic peril. Should that happen, we might wind up depluralizing our polity and, over the long run, endangering our democracy in order to "save" it. That, at any rate, would be a worst-case scenario as one connects up historic forces and developments to contemporary trends.

In his recent book, *The Dissent of the Governed: A Meditation on Law, Religion, and Loyalty,* the distinguished constitutional scholar Stephen Carter reminds us that tolerance "is not simply a willingness to listen to what others have to say. It is also a resistance to the quick use of state power—the exclusive prerogative of violent force, remember—to force dissenters and the different to conform." As an example of this phenomenon, Carter points to pro-life protest and the ways in which attempts to quash this form of public advocacy have proceeded apace with the blessing of the courts in applying RICO racketeering statutes against dissenters. Whether one accepts Carter's example as valid or not, his more general point is that if we set up as paradigmatic the view that the nation must be morally more or less the same, plurality is denied and community autonomy is eroded. All of this is traceable to the old notion that human beings cannot simultaneously embrace dual (or more) loyalties that may, at times, conflict. But a strong, well-ordered, free nation shouldn't fear conflict so much. Destructive division, yes. But dissent and a culture of argument—that is the very stuff of democracy, and religious pluralism guarantees there will always be such. Religion is a public institution, not a private club. The faithful person's "I believe" is said in the context of the "we" of a faith community. Those who believe may feel the call to evangelize or to counter the culture on the grounds of faith based dissent. That, too, is the stuff of a robust democracy. As the great Frederick Douglass observed, you can't have gardens and spring flowers without a bit of thunder and lightning from time to time.

The Present in Light of the Past: Where Do We Go from Here?

We live in a skeptical if not disillusioned era. We know that, on the best available evidence from our leading social scientists, Americans have withdrawn in huge numbers from hands-on civic engagement. Especially troubling is growing evidence that those most cynical about our prospects, *particularly* politics and government, are the young, with high school students the most "turned-off" of all. This is a complex phenomenon, no doubt. But I suspect that one factor in the triumph of cynicism is the fact that young people are too often fed stories that represent American history as nothing but a tale of failed promises. In an attempt to be more critical, and not to instill in our young people a simplistic and too-benign view of our past, some have gone overboard in the other direction. If this is true of our civic story, it pertains as well to our narratives about American religious history where we have been treated to so many accounts of the marginalization of this group or the maltreatment of another that we lose sight of the millions of Americans whose commitments to their churches lifted them up, sustained hope and faithfulness, and helped to form them as good stewards and responsible members of their communities. Everyone knows by now that both civically and religiously we have too often failed to live up to our premises and promises. But the staccato repetition of the dark side of our history, if that becomes the dominant motif, fuels cynicism rather than active participation. Let's look, then, at contrasting models of how to treat the history of religion and public life in America.

Model One: The Traditional Story

My then–five year old granddaughter told me her version of the traditional story shortly before Thanksgiving 1999. It went like this.

Grandma, we learned about Thanksgiving and why we have turkeys. The Pilgrims got on a boat called the *Mayflower* because the king wouldn't let them be free. They couldn't pray free. So they got on the *Mayflower,* and then they sailed for a long time across the ocean to come to America. Some pilgrims got sick and died. The pilgrim children had to sleep on the hard wood floors on the ship. They thought they'd never get there. But they did! It was cold and they were hungry. They got to be friends with the Indians and they shared some turkeys and some corn and gave thanks and that's why we eat turkey and have Thanksgiving, because then the Pilgrims could pray free.

This isn't a bad story, and it is essentially the one many of us were taught. It is a baseline from which to work. The story gets more complex over time, of course. The encounter with the indigenous people is, we come to understand, one with many layers of tentative coming together, suspicion, failures and successes of communication: pathos aplenty. We are familiar with how this proceeds. Jump-starting the civic formation of children with a strong, decent story seems appropriate. One could not, and no responsible parent or teacher would, offer a benign version of the coming of slavery in America. But one could tell even this horrific tale in a way that emphasized the strength of the African slaves and their determination to try to hold onto their dignity even under conditions of slavery, their valiant efforts to sustain families, their cultural contributions even enslaved.

The problem with the traditional story is if it gets reified and frozen. An example I give in my book, *Democracy on Trial,* is that of the teacher who turns the story of the Founding Fathers into an exercise in hagiography and the Constitution into a nigh-miraculous distillation of the essence of the wisdom of the ages, good for all times and places. If uncritical adulation triumphs, the dialogic, deliberative, and critical dimensions of civic engagement, an encounter that is always both retrospective and prospective, are lost. A traditional story of the reified sort about American religion would present it as a cheery tale of beleaguered folks seeking to "pray free"—true enough—but then go on to envelop the entirety of our religious history in a kind of roseate haze that overlooks the vituperation meted out against religious dissenters, the often violent exclusions, the organized attacks (here again the Know-Nothings or the Ku Klux Klan who were anti-Catholic and anti-Jewish as well as anti-black), the pretense that the common or public schools were solely a generous and benign effort to educate all American young people, thus sanitizing the effort and neglecting the explicit anti-immigrant, anti-Catholic thrust of the common schools, and so on. The good, the bad, and the ugly must be part of the story without any single element dominating, for that would be to distort through gross oversimplification. Thus there is a traditional model narrative that illuminates, another that narrows and distorts.

Model Two: The Hermeneutics of Suspicion Ascendant

The hagiographer's mirror image is offered by the teacher who, if the founding is the reference point, declares that nothing good ever came from the hand of that abstract, all-purpose villain, the "dead, white European male." The words and deeds of the Founders were nefarious as they were hypocritical racists and patriarchalists. It follows that their creations, including the Constitution, are tainted. The key words in this negative scenario are "nothing but" for these two little words always signify a reductionistic agenda. Within the rigidities of this model, debate similarly ends or is discouraged. To express a different point of view, to say maybe there were some courageous, brilliant, good things that emerged from the hands of the complex and quite various men who made so much of our early history, is to betray one's own "false consciousness" or class or race privilege. If a hermeneutics of suspicion goes all the way down that invites contemporary cynicism, especially among students.

Turned against religion, a harsh hermeneutics of suspicion sees "nothing but" patriarchy, horror, and hypocrisy at work. But here, too, there is much to be gleaned and learned. There is a version of the mode of critical interpretation that is vital and necessary in offering up a complex, nuanced, rich tapestry that affords ways for us to ask such questions as: are there resources internal to this religious tradition that enable one to criticize followers of the religion who are acting (so they say) on their religious beliefs but are, in fact, betraying those beliefs in a fundamental way? One can ask what textual distortions, ellisions, excisions, and selective use or abuse of history are required in order, for example, to draw upon the New Testament for a defense of chattel slavery even as other Christians decried slavery as a sin, and it is this latter interpretation that carried the day. Looking closely at such examples, one can readily see that this is by no means a case of two equally valid interpretations and one just opts one way or another depending on whether one is a good or bad person. Rather, one can readily see that those who found support for race based chattel slavery in the New Testament systematically bowdlerized the message of Jesus of Nazareth in order to make the message fit with the institution they sought to defend. The best response to such claims is to go to the New Testament itself and to show how such distortions had occurred. There are times when persons of good will and shared faith will differ, and there is no knock-down way to adjudicate based on tradition or on what a critical hermeneutics yields. But there are other times when the course will be clear and the critical interpretation will have made it so. Thus, this model in its balanced, not extreme, form is necessary.

Model Three: Civic and Hopeful

The civic and hopeful stance is one that draws upon elements from the traditional and critical interpretive models, then intermingles them with a strong civic philosophy to which a faith community brings robust beliefs that may well challenge or put pressure upon an extant scheme of things. Within the Christian tradition, for example, believers are called not to conform to the world but to be formed in such a way that they can transform the world. The world is wounded in so many ways: by nationalism, racism, violence. Beginning with the dignity of each and every human person, the civic and hopeful model lifts up human dignity by recognizing the religious dimension of every person: that we are made in God's image. (Other traditions would have their own starting points in response to a wounded world.) The critical-hopeful model promotes a dialogue between faith and culture and civic struggles, striving to prevent the final triumph of the highly individualistic, isolating, and excessively consumer-commercial spirit of the age as citizens are enjoined to think, to speak, and to act toward a common good. The history of American religion as a mainstay of American public life is, at its best, a story of the struggle to ask, to answer, and to attempt to achieve a good that we can know in common that we cannot know alone.

Notes

[1]Of course, this free exercise has by no means been robustly evident from our Plymouth Colony inception. But the seeds for free exercise were early sown with the Puritan emphasis on conscience. Disestablishment in Virginia would be an

early marker of established disestablishment that, of course, now pertains.

[2]Kelly (1984), p. 3.

[3]Witte (2000), p. 44.

[4]Witte (2000), p. 45.

[5]The listing of the three great Abrahamic traditions isn't meant to be exhaustive of religious expression in America, of course, but I here refer to those religions that take a congregational or "institutional" form and that have their own versions of what might be called a "constitution."

[6]The dividing line usually is traced from several Supreme Court cases that applied the First Amendment religious clauses to state and local governments leading to the emergence of a national law on religious liberty. On this see Witte (2000), p. 87.

[7]Tocqueville (1969), p. 443.

[8]Tocqueville (1969), p. 448.

[9]On "Social Contract or a Public Covenant?" see Lovin (1987), p. 135.

[10]Lovin (1987), p. 288.

[11]Cathy Lynn Grossman, "In Search of Faith," *USA Today* (December 23–26, 1999), pp. 1–2. The article contends that people prefer to be seen as "spiritual" rather than "religious." But, as Bishop Wilton Gregory of Belleville, Illinois, vice president of the National Conference of Catholic Bishops, noted: "What do they mean by 'spiritual'? That they watched two episodes of 'Touched by an Angel'?" It seems so. One fellow is quoted saying he gets as much out of a long bike ride as he does going to church. Bike rides apparently clear the mind. But religion isn't supposed to clear the mind; it is supposed to fill it up with convictions, beliefs, creeds, hymnody, sacred texts, the sharing of what is deep and purposeful.

[12]Allen (2000), p. 14 typescript.

[13]Please note that a consideration and critique of *philosophical liberalism* by no means implies that the critic is either politically a "liberal" or a "conservative." Both political liberals and conservatives in America are indebted to the philosophically liberal tradition. Only the accents vary, for the most part. In other words, there are very few conservatives of the sort that trace their ancestry to Edmund Burke. American conservatism at this point is far more likely to be a variant on market models of individual liberty.

[14]Many of the fights over intolerance toward authentic religious pluralism that includes Catholics are directly traceable to Protestant-Catholic battles that began in the nineteenth century. Americans United for Separation of Church and State, for example, was originally Protestant and Other Americans United for Separation of Church and State. Many of us recall reading the fulminations of Paul Blanchard and others about the threat to American democracy from Catholicism. I recall that in 1960 when, as a person who couldn't yet vote (the voting age was yet eighteen), I worked the precincts for John F. Kennedy for president, and I was actually chased out of a person's living room as that determined woman wielded a Bible as a weapon, screaming as she did so that the election of a Catholic would be "the Pope in the White House." No one familiar with the history of American prejudice should assume that this particular animus has vanished. As well, it should be noted that many of the arguments once made against Catholics are now mounted against followers of Islam: they really cannot be loyal Americans, theirs is an alien creed, and so on.

[15]Lovin (1986), p. 141.

[16]On this see Witte (2000), p. 97.

[17]Other scholars speak of a move to "secular establishment" through the courts. See Gary D. Glenn and John Stacks, "Is America Safe for Catholicism," *The Review of Politics* (winter 2000), pp. 5–29.

[18]Here a key text is Rawls (1993). Rawls excludes religiously grounded moral arguments from political discourse on grounds of "unreasonableness."

[19]Carter (1998).

2

Standing at the Precipice: Faith in the Age of Science and Technology

Azizah Y. al-Hibri

We discussed earlier that strand of European liberalism that reached our shores and influenced our constitutional views on the separation of church and state. This tradition was based on several assumptions. As pointed out, among them is the assumption that individuals could seal themselves off into compartments to be believers one moment, good citizens the next. Another is the assumption that religion is retrograde, that it will be overtaken by reason. These assumptions fit well with certain secular assumptions of modern science, especially when combined with the mech-

AZIZAH Y. AL-HIBRI is professor of law at the T.C. Williams School of Law at the University of Richmond, founding editor of *Hypatia: a Journal of Feminist Philosophy*, and founder and vice president of KARAMAH: Muslim Women Lawyers for Human Rights. She is author of a book on deontic logic and many articles on Muslim women's rights, democracy, and human rights. She is a member of the editorial board of *The Journal of Law and Religion* and *The American Journal of Islamic Social Sciences*, contributing editor of *Second Opinion*, and member of the Board of Advisors of The Religion and Human Rights Series at Emory University. Dr. al-Hibri is also a member of the Advisory Board of the Pluralism Project at Harvard University and Religion and Ethics NewsWeekly for PBS.

anistic model of reality on which the Industrial Revolution was based.[1]

The mechanistic model of the Industrial Revolution has thoroughly permeated not only our technological world, but more importantly, our very consciousness, even subconsciousness. It has structured our worldview and cast its shadow over every aspect of our lives. It has also shaped our fundamental assumptions. Our view of scientific thought, professional behavior, medicine, business, education, even religion has been influenced by it. Divisions on the Supreme Court in the debates over the separation of church and state clearly reflect it. The consequences, both positive and negative, have been immense. Dehumanization, fragmentation, and conflict are among the most troubling. For people of faith in particular, it has meant a schizophrenic existence. It has legitimated a separation of faith from public life, causing an unfortunate rupture that marginalized faith as it privatized one's deepest-held beliefs and values.

At the cusp of the second millennium, however, a new age has dawned upon us. It is the Age of Information that emphasizes interconnectedness, decentralization, and innovation. This new age tends to promote an organic as opposed to a mechanistic reality. It abandons a hierarchical mechanistic logic in favor of "flattened" networks of relationships. It replaces the ideology of conflict that characterized the Industrial Age with a new ideology of cooperation. It replaces homogeneity with diversity, and centralization with increased participation and democracy. Properly understood and managed, this age can usher in better political, social, and economic relations in our society and in the world.[2] Left in chaos, it could result in the disarray of our various institutions.

Our generation is in the unique position of being able to either birth this new age or suppress its development by forcing it into outmoded First Industrial molds. We have been raised in the Old World, but history demands from us that we define the contours of the New World. In some sense, our task is no less critical than that of our Founding Fathers who ushered in a new era of liberation and democracy into a world burdened with oppression and tyranny. Thus we must engage in serious deliberations, taking into account our true state of affairs, before we reach our conclusions.

In launching his extensive critique of our mechanical technological culture, Marshall McLuhan, the oracle of this new age, noted in *The Gutenberg Galaxy* that "[h]itherto most people have accepted their cultures as fate . . .; but our emphatic awareness of the exact modes of many cultures is itself a liberation from them as prisons." We need not be prisoners of our old mechanistic culture, and in fact have been slowly liberating ourselves from it. But to properly plan for and accelerate the future, we need to understand the past. We need to uncover the impact certain unwarranted assumptions underlying the mechanistic models have had on us, not only in industry but also socially, politically, and legally. Indeed, these assumptions have so permeated our lives that they have become practically invisible.

The Story of Modern Science and Technology

Faith and reason have been juxtaposed in theological and philosophical discussions for centuries, sometimes with reason portrayed as the handmaiden of religion but at others, as polar opposites. These discussions have not always been cordial. They flourished and took new forms during the European Renaissance and Enlightenment. Finally, they reached the shores of this land during and after the American Enlightenment.

Today, the issues raised by these discussions have shifted in great part to areas related to science and technology, but the discussions remain as vibrant as ever.[3] The issues permeate all aspects of our American life from educational and artistic arenas to constitutional and political ones. Often, however, people of faith have been disadvantaged in these discussions precisely because the image of science and technology in the public square is one of "secularity," "objectivity," and "provability," while religious belief continues to be commonly cast as "superstitious," "irrational," and "private."

This situation is not conducive to a dialogue based on equality and mutual respect, and has alienated important segments of our society from each other. In part, this state of affairs is the result of the great successes of modern science and the notable excesses of some groups and individuals in the name of faith. Unfortunately, however, our great admiration for science has led to its mystification, and has endowed it with unjustified *secular political authority*. In a way, science has become the new religion. This development has created problems even for scientific researchers. It threatens to hinder further scientific progress and undermine our system of democracy;[4] therefore, in the next few paragraphs, I shall highlight some vulnerabilities of modern science in order to accelerate better science, greater innovation, and a vigorous democracy.

It is important to remember that science has not always adopted a secular point of view. Many of the basic elements in the foundation of modern science and technology were laid in medieval times by Islamic scholars such as Jaber Ibn Hayyan, al-Khawarizmi, Ibn al-Haitham, and Ibn Sina (Avecinna). None of these scientists recognized a conflict between reason (whether deductive or inductive) and faith. In fact, they recognized a deeper spiritual reality and believed firmly that God created the world according to specific laws. It was their task to discover these laws as proof of the wonders of God. Their approach, which was also based on experimentation and observation, arranged the metaphysics of Islamic science on the basis of faith.

Modern science has other spiritual origins. For example, the regular measurement of time was an important element of the budding industrial world. In fact, some view the mechanical clock as the key machine of the Industrial Age. Very early on, monasteries of the West, with their time-sequenced bells and orderly routine, provided an early example of the ordered life and the orderly universe created by God. For this reason, some authors have even argued that the Industrial Age derived its mechanical conception of time in part from the routine of the monastery. Furthermore, many monks were among the early scientists. In fact, Roger Bacon was a monk; so was Gregor Mendel. These observations provide a useful perspective for understanding Alfred Whitehead's emphasis on the importance of scholastic belief in a universe ordered by God to the foundations of modern physics.

Even our Founding Fathers seem to have viewed faith and reason as allies. For example, Thomas Jefferson, who was quite interested in science and technology, was accused by his opponents of atheism. Nevertheless, in a letter to Peter Carr in 1787, Jefferson told him that "[y]our own reason is the only oracle given you by heaven, and you are answerable not only for the rightness but uprightness of the decision." In a letter to David Barrow in 1815, Jefferson also stated that "[w]e are not in a world ungoverned by the laws and the power of a superior agent."

Today's science, popularly conceived as "secular," "objective," and "provable," actually makes unprovable metaphysical assumptions. This is one reason that, despite undeniable successes, the scientific image has come recently under attack from within the scientific and philosophical communities. Some scientists have pointed to the selectivity of data gathered and the subjectivity of the scientist as real problems in developing an "objective" scientific theory.[5] That is, scientific data are often distorted by human consciousness. Others have pointed to unwarranted assumptions made by scientists, such as the denial of intelligent design in the universe. Charles Townes, the Nobel Prize winning physicist and chief inventor of the laser, noted that "[p]ositing that essential features of the natural world are explained by billions of variables that cannot be observed strikes me as much more freewheeling than any of the church's claims."[6] Townes represents a growing trend among modern scientists to question the secular biases of science.[7]

Also, feminists have charged traditional scientists with patriarchal bias in the gathering of data and development of theories.[8] For example, Ruth Bleier argues that otherwise-good scientists "have shown serious suspensions of critical judgment in interpretations of their own and others' data." They have "ignored the known 'complexity and malleability of human developments' to make 'unsubstantiated conjectures' not one of which 'is known to be descriptive of scientifically verifiable reality as we know it today.' "[9]

For this reason, Elizabeth Lloyd and others argue that it makes for *better* science "to encourage the training and full participation of informed researchers with a variety of background experiences, preconceptions, and viewpoints, precisely because such inclusion will encourage a wider variety of working hypotheses as well as a more thorough challenge and testing of any given scientific hypothesis or theory under consideration.[10] The object therefore is not to discredit science, but to "demystify" it and make it more exact.[11] This can only be done by undermining the *social and political authority* of science that attempts to shield its shortcomings from public view and opening up the field for informed, intelligent, and demo-cratic exchange of ideas.[12]

Despite its spiritual roots, modern science blossomed on funda-mentally secular mechanistic assumptions for which there was no conclusive proof. A truly scientific attitude would have left the door open for entertaining all workable possibilities. As a result, science has often been reduced to "scientism," that is, an ideological tool based on views not fully supported by data. As the result of these unwarranted assumptions, new alternative theories continue to struggle hard for acceptability in our scientific society. Three recent examples in the area of medicine come to mind: spirituality, acupuncture, and holistic medicine. Only recently, and most likely as a result of patient pressure, did the medical profession finally de-cide to take a serious look at them.[13] As a result, significant progress recently has been achieved.

As these examples illustrate, the real problem with ideologically biased scientific attitude is that it could slam the door in the face of valuable future innovation. Worse yet, it would continue to em-bolden harmful attitudes within and toward humanity. To avoid these consequences, we need to introduce to the world of science, as we did to our society, the concept of "diversity," in this case, in-tellectual diversity. We also need to legitimize the language of spir-ituality in the halls of science to the extent that unwarranted secular metaphysical assumptions are being made.

In the Information Age, human capital is more important than financial capital. So we need to train our children in the art and sci-ence of critical reasoning. It is appalling how little training in this area our children receive before they reach college. As a result, they are unable to evaluate properly much of the unsupported secular scientific and other information directed at them at an early age. This educational defect breeds a generation of automatons who in-ternalize uncritically whatever is given to them, an unacceptable state of affairs in a country that values freedom of thought and democracy.

Furthermore, recent studies about innovation and the Informa-tion Age show that new structures based on intellectual openness, cooperation, and a vigorous exchange of ideas are fueling the re-markable accomplishments in Silicon Valley.[14] So vigorous is this exchange of ideas that many no longer attach much significance to trade secrets. The result has catapulted our country to the forefront of world development. Given these data that support intellectual openness and organizational democracy in the interest of innovation, there is no excuse for the continued sequestering of science from ideologically "unpopular" ideas, such as those rooted in feminist, environmentalist, spiritual, or faith perspectives.

Further, the values of cooperation and promotion of communal interest reflected in Silicon Valley are important values traditionally advocated by faith communities. These are clearly to be contrasted with the values prevalent among employees in highly competitive hierarchical corporations or scientists competing for funding in traditional institutions.

The Broken Promises of Science, Technology, and Religion

I have argued that "closing" the scientific mind to other promising ways of looking at the world undermines democracy, suffocates innovation, and harms society. I have examined the first two claims and turn now to the third.

The benefits to society of scientific and technological innovation are obvious, but they have not measured up to expectations. Despite unprecedented wealth, our country has eliminated neither poverty nor homelessness. Millions of American children and senior citizens still go to bed hungry, and an even larger number has no medical insurance. Furthermore, industrialization has sprouted its own local and global problems.

For example, until punitive laws were passed, producers adulterated bread to increase their margins of profit, and manufacturers operated sweatshops for children. In the 1970s companies that sold infant formula used aggressive marketing methods in Third World countries, despite the fact that placing a baby on the bottle there was often hazardous to its health and at times resulted in death. These days, genetic engineering, which promises to eliminate certain illnesses, has been used in agricultural research to produce terminator seed, i.e., seed genetically designed to render second-generation seed sterile. This means that farmers can no longer save seed from their harvest. They have to purchase it from an increasingly concentrated global market of seed companies. This development will spell even greater trouble to the beleaguered American small farmer.

Also, free trade and the globalization of business have been viewed as having a negative effect on workers' wages, whether in the Third World or in industrialized countries. It is these kinds of concerns that finally led to the angry demonstrations in Seattle during the World Trade Organization's meeting, and protests against the International Monetary Fund and the World Bank in Washington.[15] The Frankenstein monster appears to have gone out of control. Workers, farmers, environmentalists, and other concerned individuals in the United States and around the world are simultaneously angry and scared.

The voices of the people of faith in the United States on these issues have been relatively muffled and fragmented. The loudest argument being heard is about the "height" of the wall between church and state as described in Supreme Court cases. It appears that many people of faith have internalized the arguments for market efficiency, maximization of profit, and preserving our "superpower" status. Many religious institutions have in fact benefited greatly from their business investments. This situation has created a "shared vision" between corporations and shareholders, many of whom are people of faith and religious institutions. This shared material vision has unfortunately often dulled spiritual sensibilities.

People of faith need to reexamine their priorities as well as their basic assumptions. We need, for example, to reflect on the legal proposition that the duty of corporate directors is to maximize shareholder wealth. In the 1980s, many older employees lost their jobs and were left unemployable in a process called "downsizing" designed to maximize shareholder wealth. The wave of mergers and acquisitions that made many shareholders very wealthy often resulted in bankruptcies that harmed the interests of creditors and employees. As a result, stakeholder statutes were enacted in many states permitting directors to consider interests of other stakeholders in a company, such as creditors and employees, in reaching their final decision.

These stakeholder laws and subsequent thinking on corporate

legal reform originated from concerned citizens, many of whom do not have a clear religious affiliation or motive, and some of whom may in fact be nonbelievers in God but believers in humanity and decency.[16] Until recently, people of faith and their institutions defined their domain of responsibility very narrowly, confining it to general moral pronouncements with no concrete solutions in professional or other specialized areas of knowledge. As a result, they have marginalized themselves in this society and have been viewed as old fashioned and irrelevant to solving the problems of the modern world. This state of affairs has begun to change and must change if we truly believe in the relevance of faith to the modern world.

Fragmented and Compartmentalized Existence

The mechanistic model of the First Industrial Revolution continues to dominate our society today despite the fact that many branches of science have abandoned that model. We have borrowed this outmoded model and embedded it in various aspects of our lives. Now it is time for us to catch up with our future possibilities. This demands a conscious critique of the ways in which the mechanistic model has been embedded in our culture, and how it has affected our lives.

The model gives rise to the mechanistic approach that consists of reducing entities into their components and then isolating these components to study them in great detail. In other words, under this approach an entity is equal to the sum of its parts. There is no recognition of an organic whole that could transcend the sum of these parts. Despite the fact that the mechanistic model and related approach have become obsolete in the Information Age, our universities, corporations, hospitals, and social and other institutions continue to be organized in accordance with them.

In the field of modern business, we view a corporation as the basic building block. It is kept in good operation by a balance of power among directors, officers, and shareholders. In determining corporate policies, the board of directors is expected to restrict itself to determining what is best for the corporation and its shareholders. Such is the proper professional attitude. The effect of such policies on the community or the country is beyond the scope of matters considered by the board except to the extent it may adversely affect the image of the corporation in the community and hence its profits.

Decades ago, the philosopher Erich Fromm pointed out that today's notions of efficiency are defined too narrowly. What is an efficient policy for a corporation may not be efficient for the community or the country as a whole. In that case, he was referring to a policy by a phone company of monitoring telephone operators. He argued that such monitoring is bad for operators, engendering in them feelings of inadequacy, anxiety, and frustration. Hence this policy is ultimately bad for the community. Today, monitoring has become commonplace, and the harm to workers' psyche is no longer a major concern.

Law reflects a similar approach of fragmentation and compartmentalization. Corporate law, for example, deals with corporate governance issues and shareholder interests. It leaves out totally an important part of the corporation, namely the employees. To find out about these, we have to enter a whole new field, that of labor law. By fragmenting discussion in this fashion, we have a distorted perspective of what constitutes good policies for the corporation and what maximizes wealth. Had we put the two areas together, we could have discovered quickly, for example, that certain policies would reduce worker loyalty and lead to a drop in production and profitability. Individuals who support better integrated corporate policies that take into account societal interests are often viewed as "soft" and ineffective.

Our large firms are often organized in ways that do not recognize sufficiently the existence of the family. Associate lawyers on Wall Street may work twenty hours a day. Resident doctors in large cities may be on call every other night. We are told that such grueling schedules ensure excellent professional training. In fact, they raise the margin of profit for the employer, while shifting the human and financial costs of this policy to the employees, their clients or patients, and their families. The prolonged working hours of the employees render them more susceptible to error and make their families feel burdened and abandoned. This unfortunate state of affairs is partly the reason for our high divorce rate and the increase in the number of troubled children. These profit-maximizing policies may benefit the firm or hospital, but they result in a world where humanity is degraded, emotional ties are frayed and withered, and humans are disposable and fungible.

Even in matters of faith, we have internalized this defective mechanistic model. Our lives are often viewed as consisting of two components, the public and the private. Our beliefs are also viewed as a collection of component beliefs, one of which may be religious. Given the bias against religion in the public space, we have learned to leave the religious component to the private space. True, many politicians have been using religious public language nowadays to further their political goals, but in doing so they have devalued religious language in the public square. Significantly, they also stirred a great deal of controversy when they were earnest about their statements.

Many of us believe that under the "common language" approach it is possible to find common ground among believers and nonbelievers. This can be done by simply focusing on nonreligious component beliefs and by using nonreligious "common" public language, i.e., language from which expressly religious terms and ideas have been expunged.[17] Now, as the Williamsburg Charter makes clear, "civility obliges citizens in a pluralistic society to take great care in using words and casting issues.[18] But that does not mean that religious language must be expunged from conversation in the public square. Indeed, there are times when expunging it actually leads to loss of both information and effective communication.

For example, we can all agree that democracy is essential because we all agree to our constitutional principles. It is not important for us to know, however, that Sam's agreement is rooted in his Christian view that God created us all equal, whereas, John's is rooted in his secular liberal beliefs. That is viewed as superfluous information that, if explored, may bring out serious differences. But this preference for "surface information" impoverishes the national dialogue at times, imperils it at others, and reduces every individual to a "black box." It measures success by individual outcomes without developing a real feel for what may be happening under the surface. In the past, this absence of effective communication has led to polarization, and even violence.[19] To describe the "surface information approach" in engineering terms, it could build bridges on shaky, unexplored grounds rendering them vulnerable to collapse when placed under stress. For this reason, it is important to balance the need for a common language with the need to express certain important ideas in one's own faith language. Perhaps ultimately we may even be able to weave the two alternatives successfully together.

Just as significant is the fact that by asking persons of faith to reconstruct their language and arguments in the public square, we are placing upon them unique burdens not shared by their secular friends. Persons of faith presenting an argument in the public square will now have to redesign it, remold it, and reconfigure it in order to have it make sense to a secular audience. They may or may not succeed in this attempt. If they miss, their contribution will be used as yet another example of how people of faith are biased, retrograde, and make no sense. Their secular counterparts usually have no such burdens placed upon them. They can say exactly what they think. They do not need to reconfigure and reshape their arguments in order to appeal to a religious public square. This state of affairs damages democracy by creating two types of citizens: one defines acceptable public language and ideas; the other has to comply with that definition. This is why many people of faith feel like second-class citizens in these United States.

Other aspects of the secularized public square place additional stress and burdens on committed people of faith. Because of their worldview and its attendant values that preach cooperation, honesty, and egalitarianism, committed people of faith in particular will find the values of the modern workplace intolerable. This is not to argue that some secularists do not experience similar conflicts, but rather that the worldview of committed people of faith is inherently in conflict with the values of today's workplace. On the other hand, secularist values and worldviews vary widely, and some do not engender these types of inherent conflicts.

We have already spoken about the intense competitive climate and rigid hierarchical structure in many American corporations. We now turn to specific examples. In advertising, whether employee or employer, the person of faith has to please the client. This involves at times promoting questionable products, such as cigarettes, and defective products, such as car models that have a propensity to overturn. In the area of health care, an HMO employee may find himself or herself in the position of having to deny many medical claims that he or she would otherwise have accepted but for the over-reaching profit-maximizing policies of the HMO. In law, the partner or associate is bound by the adversarial system to seek the best, but not necessarily the fairest, arrangement for the client. In government, an elected official is often beholden to his or her financial supporters not his or her conscience.

Surely, a person of faith can reject all these traps, but then there are not too many options left for earning a living. As a result, the person of faith will have to develop either a schizophrenic personality or a maladjusted one. In the first case, he or she would live the secular life during the working days of the week and the religious life over the weekend. His or her two lives would be out of touch with or irrelevant to each other. In the second case, he or she can refuse to lead a fragmented existence, thus feeling oppressed, anguished, alienated, and unhappy. Such an individual radiates unhappiness to those around him or her.

Most of us try to straddle the two alternatives by opting for unhappiness sometimes, denial at other times. But we never have a real opportunity to live the spiritually integrated life we desire. Secularists who are not committed to values similar to ours experience no such conflicts. This alone is sufficient to show that the public square is not neutral between religionists and nonreligionists. It is significantly slanted in favor of secular ethics that conflict with our own. But we are prohibited from critiquing these values, because we cannot bring our religious beliefs openly and honestly to the public square. Instead, we have to search for innocuous (nonreligious, even nontheist) common language that would express our critique without divulging the heart of the conflict. How did we get to this point, when the Founding Fathers were theists who strongly believed in a Creator? To answer this question, we need to take a quick look at the handiwork of the Supreme Court over the past few decades.

Separation of Church and State

The mechanistic approach of compartmentalizing religion lends support to the Supreme Court's attempt to erect a high wall of separation between church and state. For this reason, it is useful to highlight some of the mechanistic assumptions about the world and the nature of belief that appear to undergird certain Supreme Court opinions.

According to some justices, the establishment clause embodies the view that religion "must be a private matter for the individual, the family, and the institutions of private choice." But, as argued earlier, it does not make sense to tell people of faith to cabin their faith to the privacy of their own sphere, for their faith is not just one more component of their set of beliefs. It is rather an integral part of their worldview. The real issue is not about cabinning one's faith, but rather about ways of sharing one's faith perspective in the public square without coercion or acrimony. In the age of pluralism in America, the challenge to develop new ways of communicating and interacting is urgent. Mechanistic assumptions and solutions only serve to deny the problem and delay its resolution.

A proper understanding of the establishment clause is especially significant today, where the governmental public square has expanded considerably. This expansion provides new grounds for arguing today that since the American Constitution has guaranteed for people of faith the right to freedom of conscience, then they should be able to exercise that freedom openly in the governmental public square, side by side with those who are not people of faith.[20] Otherwise, the right of people of faith to free exercise would be severely limited. Recently the Court wrestled with this issue yet one more time, trying to balance the right of people of faith to free exercise with the Court's concern about the coercive majoritarian policies and the appearance of governmental establishment of religion.[21]

The Supreme Court has articulated several different approaches to the establishment clause and the separation of church and state. Three major approaches, which will be discussed below, have come to be known as "strict separationism," "endorsement," and "accommodationism."[22]

Strict Separationism

The first approach views religion and government as two separate "spheres" that should not be permitted to interfere or be "mixed" with each other. These interpretations are clearly influenced by the mechanistic view that assumes the possibility of such sequestering. It takes the "wall of separation" imagery used by Jefferson perhaps too literally. This approach is rooted in the historical conflicts of this nation and not in hostility toward religion.

Separatists trace their views to Jefferson, Madison, the Baptists, and others. Our Founding Fathers were theists who wanted the state to stay out of the church's business. Coming from a European background, they were only too familiar with state oppression resulting from the adoption by the state of an "official" religion, and then using that as a tool to oppress others. In fact, some Founding Fathers were already aware of serious examples of religious intolerance in their own backyard in Virginia.

The travails of Baptists, such as John Weatherford, James Ireland, and John Waller, are well documented.[23] Ultimately, John Leland, the most popular Baptist preacher in Virginia, is reported to have met with Madison. As a result of this meeting, the Baptists helped elect Madison and supposedly influenced his decision to secure the First Amendment.[24] That was, of course, only part of the picture. Other parts of the country were experiencing similar problems.

It is these sorts of considerations and the commitment to freedom of conscience that led the Founding Fathers to erect a "wall of separation" to keep out the state from the affairs of the various religious communities. There is nothing in their views that leads one to conclude that they envisioned a secularized governmental public square in which religious points of view are discriminated against in favor of nonreligion.

Stripping the public square from all religious encouragement, symbols, and words does not leave it neutral; rather it leaves it secular (i.e., nontheist). By doing so, the state policy in effect favors nonreligion over religion.

This point was made very clearly by Justice Douglas in 1952 in *Zorach v. Clauson:*

We are a religious people whose institutions presuppose a Supreme Being. We guarantee the freedom to worship as one chooses. . . . When the state encourages religious instruction or cooperates with religious authorities by adjusting the schedule of public events to sectarian needs, it follows the best of our traditions. . . . To hold that it may not would be to find in the Constitution a requirement that government show callous indifference to religious groups. That would be preferring those who believe in no religion over those who do believe.

From a more philosophical perspective, the argument is much clearer. By removing all religious symbols and words from the governmental public square, it becomes one where only a nonreligious worldview is expressed. Under such worldview, God becomes a mere private option that can be added or subtracted from one's set of beliefs.

Persons of true faith cannot possibly adopt this point of view. For them, God is at the center of the universe and God defines all their relations within society and the family. God is not a private option added to their beliefs but the very center post of these beliefs. Take God out, then their system is hollow, rendering it extremely vulnerable. This state of affairs is akin to that of asking secularists to restate their views after adding to them one simple assumption, namely, the existence of God. Clearly, that one simple assumption will wreak havoc on their worldview, forcing them to reshape their arguments and remold them in ways that would be oppressive to them. If they are burdened by our demand and cannot satisfy it successfully, why should persons of faith be expected to do so instead? Given these analytic considerations, it is hard to see how our concept of neutrality does not prefer nonreligion over religion.

Legal discussions about "neutrality" rarely confronted the difficult philosophical problems engulfing the concept. Instead, judicial concepts of neutrality have been reduced to discussions of the legality of governmental "aid" to religions.[25] The more serious question, however, is not about aid. It is about the true *nature* of a framework of government that is thoroughly secular and its *impact* on our policies, domestic and foreign, on our judicial decisions, and even on the consciousness of our young generation educated within such a system. Ronald Thieman addresses this concern at length, concluding that "[w]hen under the guise of neutrality, government actually prefers one conception of the good over another, it misleads the public concerning government's roles in the adjudication of volatile moral and political matters."[26] The result is a sharpening of conflicts and a loss of trust in government.

It is also important to remember the context in which Jefferson, Madison, the Baptists, and others made their comments. The issue then was not whether the state would be theist or atheist, but rather that the state could not take sides among the various competing "sects." Further, those who did not care to take any side because they held different beliefs altogether were assured freedom of conscience. This is the import of Jefferson's statement that it neither picked his pocket nor broke his leg if his neighbor were an atheist. His neighbor can hold any belief he or she wants in this country. It does not follow, however, that Jefferson was recommending that the state emulate that neighbor in the name of "neutrality."

Additionally, we have to keep in mind that the state Jefferson was contemplating was a minimalist state in which being a member of Congress was not considered a full-time job. Today, our modern state has broken the bounds of minimalism and grown into a behemoth that has invaded numerous aspects of our society. As a result, the "governmental" public square and the "civic" one have overlapped significantly. Under these conditions, placing strict separatist restrictions on our government can only lead to the establishment of secularism in our *society* and not just in our government. If anything, the Founding Fathers, the history of this country, and the belief of the overwhelming majority of Americans today in a divine being indicate that such a development goes against the grain.

Supporters of the separationist approach tacitly admit the untenability of its strict application when they permit limited contact with religion. Accordingly, religion may be recognized by the state as an aspect of the country's history or culture. Government is permitted to use symbols or practices that have lost their religious significance. Among these some Justices have included our national motto "In God We Trust" and the reference to God in the Pledge of Allegiance.

This view raises the following question: in a country where the overwhelming majority of citizens are theists, for whom did these symbols lose their religious significance? Most likely to the secularists, otherwise they would complain about them, and the symbols would likely be removed from the governmental public square to avoid the appearance of establishment of religion. This suggests that we can bring religious symbols and practices into the governmental public square so long as the secularists declare them devoid of religious significance. Secularists then hold immense power over our governmental public square.[27] They determine what symbols may be brought into it. Religionists have no similar power. This means that we live in a state that favors nonreligion over religion.

The Endorsement Approach

This approach is less mechanistic; it is also fairer in its treatment of religion. It recognizes the increasingly wider area of intersection between church and state and permits religious expression by the state so long as it does not have the effect of endorsing religion. This means that the state may use religious symbols in holiday displays, so long as the overall display makes clear that the state does not endorse their religious significance. The endorsement view argues for equal protection among religions and between religion and nonreligion. Under this view, the state does not need to argue that a Christmas tree has become a secular symbol; it only needs to make clear that it is not endorsing its religious significance, whatever that may be.[28]

Unfortunately, the trend on the Court has been one of giving interpretations of this test that result in a strict separationist approach. For example, Justice Souter has argued that the endorsement approach, when carried to its logical conclusion, would require striking down not only graduation prayers but also traditional government practices, such as religious proclamations and religious invocations at Thanksgiving. Justice Brennan and Justice Stevens argue that the use of symbols that retain any religious meaning is unconstitutional, because it will have an endorsement effect. These interpretations of the endorsement approach suggest that fundamental questions about the nature of our government and the viability of the mechanistic separationist approach in the legal arena must be addressed.

The Accommodationist Approach

In *Allegheny v. ACLU,* Justice Kennedy argued that religious expression by the state was permissible as long as the government does not coerce participation. In other words, the state may recognize, accommodate, even support religion, so long as it does not proselytize or effectively establish or tend to establish, through direct aid for example, a state religion. Under this approach, we do not need to deny the religious significance of our national motto "In God We Trust." Nor does our public square need to lead a fragmented or compartmentalized existence. On the other hand, under this view, secularists may feel like outsiders, and even some people of faith may feel nervous, if the state consistently chooses to walk a thin line between establishment and support of a particular religion.

The best solution for dealing with these concerns is a vigorous and honest national debate. Thieman, for example, views the notion of separation as outmoded and calls for fresh jurisprudence that takes into account the original insights of Madison and is based on such fundamental values as freedom, equality, and mutual respect.[29] John Witte calls for new balances among the principles of separation of church and state, equality of plural religions, and liberty of conscience.[30] In their proposals, both authors are mindful of the concerns of minority religions and the new religious diversity in America.

Minority religions are also mindful of the possibility of the tyranny of the majority. An educated national dialogue, that is, one that has been sensitized to such matters as civility, diversity, and conflict resolution, provides valuable opportunities. It can help build reliable bridges of trust at all levels of society. It can also help us diagnose unrecognized barriers, problems, and attitudes. Those engaging in the dialogue may learn to go beyond tolerance to understanding and respect. We need to recognize that the times in which we live represent a critical era in the history of our country. If we do not try to rise to the level of sincerity, commitment, and constitutional wisdom exhibited by our predecessors, the muddled and biased *status quo* will prevail, and the next generation of Americans will pay a heavy price.

To be successful, our national dialogue must be inclusive. This means that we need to hear the concerns of secularists and have them hear the concerns of people of faith. We need to discuss with each other not just the establishment clause, but also the failure of the mechanistic strict separationist approach to life and the fact that the present state of affairs is not "neutral" and thus violates the

First Amendment. The secularists must be helped to recognize the frustration and unhappiness of many people of faith with this inequitable regime of constitutional interpretation. While fully committed to the Constitution, people of faith are no longer willing to live in this country as second class citizens nor sacrifice the moral upbringing of their children. The present regime of constitutional interpretation has led to the secularization of the public square and the relativization of values. This troubles people of faith deeply, because the next generation of Americans is already showing signs of moral distress.

We should initiate this important dialogue as soon as possible. But first, we should each take a good look at who we really are and what do we really stand for. Labels do not usually mean much. It is what is in the heart that counts. For this reason, I shall now turn to a Biblical/Qur'anic story that will shed light on a real difference between a person of faith and a nonbeliever. It cuts through labels to show that a believer is someone who does not try to be like God. Under this definition, many secular humanists exhibit, in some important sense, faith.

Adam's Modern Folly

The Bible tells us that the serpent that tempted Eve was very subtle. The divine prohibition had warned Adam and Eve against eating from the tree, "lest you die." But the serpent contradicted this divine warning and promised them that "your eyes will be opened, and you will be like God, knowing good and evil." Eve also saw that the tree "was to be desired to make one wise." She and Adam ate from the forbidden tree. The Qur'an tells us also that Satan tempted both Adam and Eve promising them eternal life and power. Adam and Eve both succumbed to this temptation.

The underlying theme of both stories is that humans desire to become divine even in the face of an explicit divine warning. That is the human folly or arrogance, for there is only one God, and we are not that God. Modern science and technology hold for today's Adam and Eve the same promise of knowledge, power, and eternal life, and despite the fact that it may destroy us ("lest you die"), Adam and Eve are not deterred.

Often authors wonder as to why the Industrial Revolution did not take place in the Ottoman Empire despite its advanced scientific and technological knowledge. There are many answers to that question, such as the absence of political and intellectual "openness." The Founding Fathers made a studied effort to avoid duplicating systems they viewed as despotic, including that of Turkey. Authors of that period also noted that there was very little free flow of information within the Ottoman Empire.

There is, however, one more factor that is worth examining. Muslim scholars were averse to spreading certain types of knowledge broadly, lest they fall in the wrong hands. For this reason, they often employed symbolisms to disguise the facts and make them accessible to only the most committed students. This cautious attitude was based on their worldview of celebrating and protecting God's creation, not replacing him. In the United States today, we have accomplished greater political and intellectual "openness" than many other societies. All types of knowledge are freely available on the Internet and in the libraries, including nuclear know-how. But the democratization of information has not been matched with widespread moral and spiritual education. As a result, we have an age in which violence, whether in inner cities, suburbs, airports, or even high schools, has become commonplace. Power has become a common idiom in communication, and violence has become the first line of argumentation.

Given this state of affairs, it is easy to understand (though not agree with) Nietzsche's declaration that God is dead, that Christian morality of meekness, humility, and charity is slave morality, and that a new breed of men has been born, that of the *Ubermensch* (superman) who is hard against himself and who must reject being merely human. The strong, Nietzsche argued, will inherit the earth. It should come as no surprise that this view was crassly appropriated by no one less than Hitler. The latter was reportedly told by the philosopher's sister that he was what her brother had in mind when he wrote about the *Ubermensch.* Freed from the burdens of Christian "slave morality," Hitler was able to scientifically annihilate millions of Jews, as well as Turks, gypsies, and others. Thus technology, without moral values, goes amok. While not every secularist is power hungry and not every person of faith is meek, the presence of faith in the public square helps anchor important moral values that many secular humanists may have very well discovered on their own.

Technology is thus a tool that the power hungry are anxious to misuse. It is in the hands of the righteous and the humane that it can fulfill its promise. But who are those? Do they include our religious leaders? History shows otherwise. History provides numerous examples of how religious individuals or institutions have used their beliefs as a tool to accumulate power, a purely selfish materialist goal. That is of course the ultimate insult to religion, i.e., using it as a tool to achieve the worst of secular goals. But that is the problem with Adam. He remains vulnerable to temptation and never gives up hope of becoming like God. In the meantime, he does the next best thing, namely, establish domination on earth, whether over nature, women, or other men.

Just as Adam was warned of destruction in the Bible, so do modern philosophers warn today's Adam as well. Herbert Marcuse, the Marxist philosopher, argued that in a society based on power and domination, the forces of Eros (love) are overpowered by the forces of Thanatos (death).[31] Unfortunately, this argument is proving only too true with the Columbine High School killings and other incidents of child violence. Our own kids are devouring themselves. In our rush to power, individually and collectively, we have destroyed the fabric of society that fosters love, affection, and interconnectedness. We have generated national anguish, anger, and hopelessness, all of which are fodder for Thanatos. In that, we are all guilty, people of faith as well as nonbelievers. Our guilt is compounded by our continued silence, as a nation, about our violence against Native Americans that destroyed many tribes and continues to harm others. We have also been silent about the violence toward Africans who were subjected to slavery and their American descendants who continue to suffer in other ways. So far, most of us have refused to publically lift the veil of silence about these issues and initiate a national dialogue for truth and reconciliation.

While the feminists fought against patriarchal domination and oppressive hierarchies, the environmentalists fought against unfettered domination and destruction of nature, and the humanists and labor unions fought for human dignity, many people of faith were often notably absent from the arena. To varying degrees many have succumbed to temptation and quietly partook of the fruits of the forbidden tree hoping that no one will notice. People of faith are the engineers, scientists, and businessmen and women of this country. Yet they go to work every day and do what is required of them, leaving religion to the weekend. This is the crux of the problem. We have compartmentalized religion and relegated faith to the role of a part-time hobby. People of faith now need to face themselves and decide the true place of faith in their lives. With our constitutional guarantees, there should be no public price paid for making a religious choice. Would such a choice, however, divide us as a nation? That is our next concern.

Civility and the Project of Finding Common Ground

The people of faith and secular humanists who are not tempted by the promise of dominion and power are likely to have a lot to talk about. Despite their different worldviews, they share a commitment to democracy, egalitarianism, and mutual respect that should make their conversations meaningful. When they reach difficult issues, they are likely to utilize helpful tools, such as further discussions, principled compromise, mediation, or methods of conflict resolution. On the other end of the spectrum, fanatic religionists and secularists would have difficulty communicating with each other and the rest of the country by virtue of their fanaticism. Their perspectives and values are based on domination, whether intellectual or physical, and domination or the attempt to dominate engenders conflict.

So for these people there is not much that we can do other than try to help them see reality and human relations in more egalitarian terms. We can achieve this end through increased public education and communication and by example. Our disagreement with them is not about religion or secularism, rather it is about democracy and power sharing, about how to respect the views of others and treat them with dignity. In this regard, recent attempts at fostering civil discourse in our public square are very important.

At the heart of the concept of civility lies the principle that we are all God's creatures, or simply that humans are endowed with dignity. Yet in our earthly existence, we have invented oppressive hierarchies, such as those of race, gender, and wealth, to differentiate us from and privilege us over others. It is these internalized hierarchies, conscious or subconscious, that provide the foundation of uncivil behavior. As members of the human race, we have consistently erected the barriers of stereotypes precisely to avoid knowing each other. When these barriers fall, each one of us will see himself or herself in that alien "other."

Incivility is not a momentary lapse. It is an outer reflection of a deep-seated belief in a system of hierarchies. This system arbitrarily bestows upon or withholds from groups of humans God's greatest gift: dignity. After all, it was God who gave dignity to the children of Adam. It is not bestowed upon us by a government, a race, or a faith. From the poorest to the richest, the youngest to the oldest, our dignity is our divine birthright.

The most oppressive form of incivility, in my view, is civil incivility, polite incivility. This occurs when the words are right but the message is wrong, when someone politely treats another as an inferior "other." This author will share a personal experience as an example. In one instance of polite conversation over coffee, my two companions were so engrossed in their conversation about Muslims that they literally forgot my presence. I guess I was not that important a member of the group to start with. To them, I was subconsciously an inferior "other." It did not require too much intellectual energy for them to first marginalize my presence, and then simply eliminate or forget it. As a result, I had the unusual experience of hearing my friends stereotype Muslims and express concerns to each other about our growing American Muslim community, but all in a very civil fashion.

Eschewing oppressive hierarchies forces us to take others seriously. If we take others seriously, then we must believe in human rights, especially the right to free expression. A view that argues against such rights contradicts my fundamental religious beliefs. Nevertheless, when faced with it, we must draw upon our faith for patience, compassion, and wisdom. We must focus on our common humanity with the other to bring down the barriers. Violence, whether verbal or physical, does not change thought. It merely suppresses it temporarily. It only hides pernicious hierarchies; it does not address them.

Each person must have room for his or her thoughts. After all, each person is directly responsible toward God (the Great Spirit, or himself/herself) for them. We also have the civic and religious responsibility to promote the values we believe in. Our faith requires us to help the society we live in be ethical. Balancing these factors, it is clear that we cannot force our values on others. We must respect their humanity, which includes freedom of thought. Hence our duty is to promote a just society in which our voices as well as other voices have a fair opportunity to be heard and in which human dignity and public welfare are carefully balanced and protected. This cannot be achieved without honesty, patience, deliberation, compassion, and even sacrifice. However, if we live by these criteria, we may not agree always, but we will certainly communicate peacefully.

What Can Concerned Citizens Do?

Concerned citizens should stop looking for easy fixes. We are at the cusp of the next millennium, and unless we give careful attention to our constitutional and societal problems, the trajectory of the U.S. rise in world leadership will be very short. To protect our country, we have to act quickly; for regardless of how fast we may act, the dialogue itself will take its own time. This is why we need to begin addressing our problems now. To do that, the following proposals may be helpful.

1. We need to take an honest look at ourselves. As Jesus said, we are quicker to find the speck in the other's eye, before we notice the log in our own eye. We, people of faith, often blame secularists for the moral problems of this country, but many of us are hypocrites who have contributed in some way to this moral decay. Some of us have embezzled funds, others have exploited the sexuality of the innocent or vulnerable, yet others have used religion as a tool for political power. In the end, many citizens have lost confidence in us. We need to earn back that confidence. To do so, we must seriously examine ourselves.

To start dealing with this situation, small neighborhood gatherings, high school and university groups, as well as religious congregations could get together in consciousness raising and bridge building meetings. At these meetings, participants could share their personal stories about serious lapses in their own behavior or judgment, lapses that conflict with their religious or moral values. Among these, for example, would be acts of race or gender discrimination, greed, or envy. The aim of the gatherings is to provide a safe zone in which various individuals could speak out honestly without being condemned or judged. The group would provide both support and direction, helping its members overcome their shortcomings by shining the light on them.

2. We need to face the past once and for all in order to reach a true reconciliation. Many argue that since slavery is obsolete, we need not dwell on the past. Generally (though not always), these voices express the point of view of the majority, i.e., those who are not the descendants of slaves. From the point of view of the latter group, there is still a lot to talk about, wounds that have not healed, truths that have not been admitted, consequences that continue to haunt us till this day. This is a festering wound, moral as well as political, in the body of the nation. We cannot cover it up with a band aid.

We need to have the courage to plunge into a national discussion about the truth of what happened then and its continuing effects today. We need to hear a diversity of voices; we need to know how racism today damages others. But we need to conduct this conversation within the framework of reconciliation and healing. To achieve this goal, careful planning for such a national conversation is necessary. Basic principles and strategies that would help launch the conversation constructively and protect it from deteriorating need to be formulated. To do that, it is helpful to examine the work of organizations already engaged in such a conversation on a limited basis.

Furthermore, great strides could be achieved if leading organizations in this country adopt this proposal and take the lead. They can plan and start the dialogue on a limited basis, until a proper formula for an effective and successful conversation has been agreed upon. In time, these organizations should plan to spread the discussion to other groups across the nation.

3. It is alright to bring our faith to all corners of the public square and make our voices heard in every arena. People of faith in law, business, medicine, education, government, and other sectors need to start thinking about how they can integrate their faith into what they do. It is alright to do so; in fact it is healthy. These individuals could also help educate us about how their faith values could inform their discipline.

Once professionals focus on these issues, they may proceed to organize meetings among them to discuss various recommendations. They may even decide to include in those meetings advisors from law, religious studies, and other areas to provide additional input. Ultimately, panels of experts may be formed consisting of people of faith from every walk of life. These panels would help develop policy positions that the rest of us would be willing to support.

For example, how should people of faith feel about the differential in income between CEOs and workers in this country? The answer is not obvious because of the many considerations involved. For one, do we help kill the goose that lays the golden egg by placing moral restrictions on corporate America? Do we care if we kill it? Who suffers the consequences? What are our priorities in this area and why?

Furthermore, if there are good arguments for paying high salaries to CEOs, because "you get what you pay for," why are these arguments confined to the corporate sector and do not cross over to the educational one? Do we not care about our children's education, and thus are not willing to pay for the best teachers, or is the field of education significantly different from that of business? Should education be organized more "efficiently" as a business, or should we be searching for a better system of organization that reflects better values and is applicable to both? These are questions in serious need of study.

4. Diversity is important and we need to express our commitment to it. We do not want a country that imprisons, tortures, or even disadvantages people who are different. The days of discrimination against the Baptists, Catholics, and others are over. We want to make sure that what happened to them does not happen to non-Christian minorities or secularists.

We need to celebrate diversity rather than dread it.

To put it in Jefferson's words:

> Let us not be uneasy then about the different roads we may pursue, as believing them the shortest, to that our last abode: but following the guidance of good conscience let us be happy in the hope that, by these different paths, we shall all meet in the end. (letter to Miles King, 1814)

If we make a deep commitment to diversity and freedom of conscience, then there will be greater cohesion among people of diverse beliefs, a broader alliance, a greater willingness to bring religion into the public square, and, generally, a more democratic state.

In this instance, it would be useful to form diverse consciousness raising groups where individuals are free to express their fears to others about discrimination in our society. In particular, I refer to religious minorities. Sometimes, the position of a minority (or even majority) group as to a public matter arises from its fear and not reason. This is not helpful to our nation in the long run. If we open safe channels for discussion, then we could assuage many of these fears. As a result, we will achieve better bases for decision making.

Again, those participating in these groups need to make a commitment to respect the views of others, regardless of how passionately they are opposed to them. Consequently, they would have to agree ahead of time on certain ground rules for civil disagreement. The case of abortion is a good illustration. Clearly, many of us have underestimated the depth of feeling of many on this issue. Participants need to agree on acceptable modes of communication that will give each side a fair opportunity to argue its case to others, and clearly delineate unacceptable behavior. For example, violence is not an acceptable method of communication. Additionally, as Americans, we all agree that our government should not discriminate against any religious view. This perhaps means that the government should be able to extend funding, where appropriate, to all religious (and secular) schools and hospitals, including in the latter case those that do or do not perform abortions, so long as there is no compelling state interest to do otherwise.

5. Our positions must be based on extensive consultation so as not to threaten others but rather make them as comfortable as possible. Consultation is the backbone of democracy. To preserve cohesion in this country, we need to consult broadly before reaching our conclusions. If difficult issues surface, experts in mediation could help us reach a fair resolution that takes all legitimate interests into account and causes no irreparable harm to any one group.

6. Our public square needs our help to flourish. As people of faith, we have a special responsibility to recognize the state of cynicism and decay that has permeated our society. If we do not deal with it soon, we will no longer have a democracy. For example, campaign finance is a moral issue that people of faith should become passionate about. We need to protect our democracy. How do we do it? Let us study the issue ourselves instead of waiting for others to propose solutions. We have experts at our table who could provide a solution emanating from our moral values. Just denouncing current practices does not help.

We also have media that have gone out of control, repeatedly beaming messages of obscenity, violence, and unabashed consumerism at our children. We need to initiate a serious dialogue about properly balancing First Amendment free speech interests with the interests of society in fostering a civil and morally acceptable public square for our children.

7. We need to foster honesty and adequate and appropriate disclosure in the public square. Many politicians are damaging the democratic underpinnings of this country by manipulating citizens to gain their votes. This has created a state of apathy that threatens to undercut our long tradition of democratic involvement. Citizens need to recapture the initiative from politicians. We can do that in many ways. For one, citizens can initiate an internal dialogue as to the types of disclosure required from politicians running for office, such as a candidate's basic history, positions, and views. They can even develop disclosure guidelines or recommended forms and lay down basic rules of engagement in the political arena, such as a requirement of civility.

This activist approach may have the effect of devaluing sensationalist efforts to invade candidates' privacy, thus opening the door to a broader range of qualified candidates. It would also help citizens make effective and informed comparisons among candidates. It is a sign of our distorted priorities that we require a disclosure document from companies selling securities on the market but not for politicians selling themselves to attain decision-making positions that could affect every aspect of our lives. If we are concerned about protecting public interest in the case of securities, why should we be any less concerned in the case of elected office?

8. Our position in the world and our role in it must be studied more seriously. Americans are "proud" of being the only superpower in the world. In fact, this is not a privilege but a burden that requires us to fulfill our calling. Unfortunately, our dealings with the world have been less than satisfactory. We have introduced to the world hedonistic values through our tools of communication. We have also made force, coercion, and sanctions building blocks of our foreign policy. As a result, we have developed a very unsympathetic image abroad. People often think that Americans are hedonist heathens. They are totally shocked to know that the Hollywood image of America is not accurate. We are paying real costs for these distortions. We need to improve communication and policy with other nations. We need to face the fact that our nation, which calls for democracy in other countries, in fact supports tyrannical regimes. This level of hypocrisy affects lives abroad and, in turn, creates anger and frustration against us. Terrorism is only one extreme expression of angry helplessness.

We need a panel of experts to study these issues, in part by traveling abroad, by consulting ethnic minorities in this country, and by gathering adequate information.

We also need as a nation to decide whether we are committed to a dialogue of civilizations as Secretary of State Madeleine Albright has asserted, or a clash of civilizations as Samuel Huntington has predicted.[32] We need to decide whether we want to usher in New World values of cooperation and community or remain captured by Old World values of conflict and domination. As people of faith, the choice should be easy, but as children of the Industrial Revolution, it may not be. The presence of an ethnically diverse group of participants with different perspectives on this issue should enlighten our discussions.

9. We need to democratize our modes of communication. The Internet has begun to do that, but our traditional modes of communication need to be examined in order to determine the extent of concentration of ownership, underlying undisclosed interests, inherent bias in data gathering, etc. We need to start a national conversation on this matter. After all, movies, video games, cable television, and regular programing are all commercial ventures that can be affected financially by public opinion. But such results cannot be achieved overnight. Expert panels must study the issues, consult, and initiate a national grassroot conversation in America's cities and towns. If there is no effective competition in these markets, then consumers can choose other strategies for increasing honesty in reporting, decreasing violence in programs and games, and making journalism a better representative of the voice of the people.

10. We need to revitalize our original democratic power. People have forgotten their original democratic power. They have let politicians, corporate entities, and taxes exhaust them. They work these days longer hours and make less money. A family must have two breadwinners to insure a decent standard of living. But many are working poor, elderly without medical insurance, and children with single or no parents. This crisis situation demands exceptional efforts for reformation. As people of faith we are called to corrective action. We need to revive the American spirit of participatory democracy in every community, on every street. For, indeed, if our democracy is at stake, then so is our liberty.

These proposals are all designed to heal the rupture in our society and in our psyches caused by a simplistic mechanistic worldview that has been partly abandoned by science and technology themselves. Open and constructive communication, based on the analysis offered in this article, will help unmask among us faulty assumptions, repressed frustrations, and deep dysfunctions that have gone so far unnoticed. I hope that it will also usher the way to a brighter future more consistent with our American tradition of cooperation, neighborliness, and robust faith.

Notes

[1]As will be argued later, early modern science did not rest on secular assumptions. Furthermore, the mechanistic model had more limited applications.

[2]For more on this new age, see Toffler and Toffler (1994).

[3]See, for example, Easterbrook (1998).

[4]For more on science's political authority and the dangers to democracy, see Lloyd (1996).

[5]See, for example, Kuhn (1970); Scheffler (1967); and Bernstein (1983).

[6]Quoted in Easterbrook (1998), p. 79.

[7]This interest is keenest in the area of medicine, where the power of prayer to heal has been under study. See, for example, "Religiosity and Remission of Depression in Medically Older Patients," *The American Journal of Psychiatry*, April 1998. See also, "Religion, Spirituality, and Medicine," *Lancet*, February 20, 1999, and the response entitled "Do Religion and Spirituality Matter in Health?" *Alternative Therapies in Health and Medicine*, May 1999.

[8]See, for example, Tuana (1996), pp. 17–35. Tuana argues: "What feminist epistemologists have realized is that it is a mistake to ask for a value-free science. . . . Scientific research, as well as all cognitive endeavors, begins with metaphysical and methodological commitments." She also states: "To say that the practice of science is marked by gender and by politics is not the same as claiming that it arises out of wishful thinking or ideological concerns. A scientific theory can provide consistent methods for obtaining reliable knowledge, yet be influenced by certain values or interests. Objectivity and neutrality are not the same thing." Tuana views the feminist critique resulting in alternative evolutionary accounts, such as "woman, the gatherer," not as a feminist "corrective" but as providing "more accurate accounts of the evidence, and . . . therefore the result of better science."

[9]Quoted in Lloyd (1996), p. 238.

[10]Lloyd (1996).

[11]For more on this, see the valuable discussion in Lloyd (1996), pp. 223–224.

[12]For more on this, see the discussion in Lloyd (1996), pp. 224–226.

[13]U.S. medical schools increasingly are offering courses in religion and spirituality. Also, the National Institutes of Health (NIH) has funded research in the area of religion, spirituality, and health. For more on this, see Larry Dossey's article in *Alternative Therapies in Health and Medicine*, May 1999.

[14]Azizah al-Hibri, "The American Corporation in the Twenty-First Century: Future Forms of Structure and Governance," *University of Richmond Law Review 31*, December 1997, pp. 1402–1409.

[15]See, for example, "Backlash: Behind the Anxiety Over Globalization," *Business Week*, April 24, 2000, especially p. 40.

[16]See, for example, Mitchell (1995).

[17]For an excellent discussion of this point, see Jean Bethke Elshtain, "How Should We Talk?" *Case Western Reserve Law Review 49*, Summer 1999, pp. 731–746.

[18]See Thieman (1996), especially pp. 168–173.

[19]Witness the heated debate, sometimes resulting in violence, on the issue of abortion.

[20]For separating out the two meanings of "public," namely, the sphere of government versus the nongovernmental sphere of civil society, see Thieman (1996), pp. 151–154. We have used here "governmental" and "civic" to express the distinction.

[21]*Doe v. Santa Fe Independent School District*. The case involved the permissibility of student initiated prayers in football games. The governmental public forum involved in this case was the public school itself. The majority opinion of the Court was troubled by the school policy that it said imposed on the student body a ma-

joritarian election on the issue of prayer. According to the Court, the school district established through this policy a "governmental electoral mechanism that turns the school into a forum for religious debate." The Court noted that "this student election does nothing to protect minority views but rather places the students who hold such views at the mercy of the majority." The dissent, on the other hand, accused the Court's opinion of "bristl[ing] with hostility to all things religious in public life."

[22]A good discussion of these approaches and others can be found in Witte (2000). Also see Kathleen A. Brady, "Fostering Harmony Among the Justices: How Contemporary Debates in Theology Can Help to Reconcile the Divisions on the Court Regarding Religious Expression by the State," *Notre Dame Law Review 75*, December 1999, pp. 509–519.

[23]See Little (1938), especially pp. 338–353, 168–191, and 53–56. See also, *The Baptists of Virginia 1699–1926* (1955).

[24]For a recent assessment of the report about the meeting, see Fred Anderson, executive director of the Virginia Baptist Historical Society, "The Leland-Madison Meeting," *Religious Herald*, March 24, 1988, p. 13, and the sequel by the same author, "This Week in Our History," March 31, 1988, p. 12.

[25]For a detailed discussion of the different articulations of the judicial concepts of "neutrality" and the question of "aid," see Thieman (1996), p. 61.

[26]Thieman (1996), p. 78.

[27]Commenting on this frustrating state of affairs, Thieman (1996) offers another critique: "Members of the judicial branch appear to be particularly ill-prepared to engage in even the minimal theological inquiry required to determine the meaning and function of a religious symbol within a religious community's vast network of beliefs and practices. Moreover, such inquiry threatens to place the 'civil magistrate' as a 'judge of religious truth,' a position Madison reckoned to be 'an arrogant pretension.' " p. 50.

[28]In fact, Justice O'Connor had no problem with the constitutionality of exhibiting a creche on government property when it was combined with secular symbols that negated any impression that the government was endorsing Christianity *(Lynch v. Donnelly)*.

[29]Thieman (1996), pp. 166–167.

[30]Witte (2000), p. 183.

[31]Marcuse (1966), pp. 86–88. While the author does not subscribe fully to the Marcusian theory, she does recognize important insights in it that are applicable to our analysis. For example, while her definition of Eros tends to be different from that of Marcuse, she nevertheless agrees with him to the extent that he defines Eros as the "life instinct" and a force that binds humanity into a closely knit mass. Eros, as used herein, is thus the love force that binds human beings into family relations and friendships. The concept of "surplus repression," i.e., that repression imposed in our society in the interest of domination, remains unchanged. Under the author's approach, an example of "surplus repression" would be excessive work hours that take parents away from their families in the interest of increasing corporate profits. Interestingly, in pursuing his analysis, Marcuse offers what sounds like a traditional critique of the increased forces of domination in our society. He states: "The technological abolition of the individual is reflected in the decline of the social function of the family. It was formerly the family which, for good or bad, reared and educated the individual, and the dominant rules and values were transmitted personally and transformed through personal fate. . . . Now, however, under the rule

of economic, political, and cultural monopolies, the formation of the mature super-ego seems to skip the stage of individualization: the generic atom becomes directly a social atom. The repressive organization of instincts seems to be *collective*, and the ego seems prematurely socialized by a whole system of extra-familial agents and agencies. As early as the preschool levels, gangs, radio, and television set the pattern for conformity and rebellion; deviations from the pattern are punished not so much within the family as outside and against the family." pp. 96–97.

[32]Madeleine Albright expressed these views in 1999 during an Iftar dinner for Muslim leaders at the State Department. Samuel Huntington has expressed his views in "The Clash of Civilizations?" in *Foreign Affairs 72:3*, Summer 1993, pp. 21–49.

3

From Battleground to Common Ground: Religion in the Public Square of 21st Century America

Charles C. Haynes

One of America's continuing needs is to develop, out of our differences, a common vision for the common good. Today that common vision must embrace a shared understanding of the place of religion in public life and of the guiding principles by which people with deep religious differences can contend robustly but civilly with each other.

The Williamsburg Charter

First presented to the nation on June 25, 1988, the Williamsburg Charter has been recognized by many commentators as a powerful and timely restatement of the religious liberty principles that undergird the First Amendment to the U.S. Constitution. Drafted by representatives of America's leading faiths and signed by nearly 200 leaders from every sector of American life, the charter calls for a national reaffirmation of religious liberty as an inalienable right—

CHARLES C. HAYNES is senior scholar at the Freedom Forum First Amendment Center. He was a principal organizer and drafter of a series of consensus guidelines on religious liberty issues in public schools endorsed by leading educational and religious organizations and is the author of *Religion in American History: What to Teach and How*. Dr. Haynes is co-author of *Finding a Common Ground: A First Amendment Guide to Religion and Public Education* and of *Taking Religion Seriously Across the Curriculum*.

and for a renewed commitment to the universal duty to guard that right for all people. The charter is built on the conviction that the religious liberty clauses of the First Amendment provide the democratic first principles that enable us to debate our differences, to understand one another, and to forge public policies that serve the common good.

Today, some twelve years after the signing of the charter and more than 200 years after the adoption of the First Amendment, America's need to articulate a "common vision for the common good" has never been more urgent—or more challenging. Our nation begins the twenty-first century as the most religiously diverse place on earth, and, among developed nations, the most religious. As the charter reminds us, the task of nation building in our time requires a shared understanding of the role religion plays in public life and a shared commitment to the core civic principles that bind us together as a people.

But how will Americans develop such an understanding and commitment across religious and ideological differences that are deep and abiding? It will not be easy. Our increasingly crowded public square is often a hostile place where citizens shout past one another across seemingly unbridgeable distances. Incendiary rhetoric and personal attacks characterize many "culture-war" debates over abortion, sex education, homosexuality, school prayer, and other hot-button issues. Any notion of the common good frequently gets lost in the crossfire of charge and countercharge. And on the fringes, wars of words can sometimes escalate into outbursts of hate and violence.

In spite of these challenges, there are at least two reasons for optimism and hope about the ability of Americans to negotiate even our deepest differences and, in many instances, to find common ground. First, as the Williamsburg Charter reminds us, the religious liberty clauses of the First Amendment—properly understood and fairly applied—provide an effective civic framework for sustaining our bold experiment in building one nation out of many peoples and faiths. And second, a number of recent civic initiatives—many involving public education—are quietly, but successfully, staking out common ground on divisive culture-war issues.

In what follows, I explore these sources of optimism, and suggest how civil dialogue might be renewed and civic consensus reached without ignoring or compromising our diverse religious and philosophical commitments.

Religion and the Public Schools

A good place to begin is public education, the perennial battleground for religious and ideological differences since the earliest days of the common school movement. From the "Bible wars" of the nineteenth century to recent fights over the posting of the Ten Commandments, conflicts over the role of religion in public schools have long divided communities, sparked bitter lawsuits, and undermined the educational mission of schools.

The struggle over religion and values in public schools has never really been about the sixty-second "to-whom-it-may-concern" prayer each morning or the Christmas tree in the school lobby. It is now and always has been a struggle over deeper questions such as "whose schools are these?" and "what kind of nation are we—will we be?" With so much at stake, it is inevitable that schools are seen as the microcosm of our public square, an arena where we debate and define who we are as a people. But when these debates degenerate into personal attacks, ridicule, false characterizations of opposing positions, and similar tactics, they tear apart the fabric of our lives together and alienate large numbers of citizens from their local schools. If we cannot find ways to negotiate our differences in public schools without going for the jugular, then the schools—and the nation—face a difficult future.

But the culture-wars in public education are not the only story. Though underreported and overlooked by much of the media, there is actually much good news coming out of many local school districts. Peaceful resolutions of many contentious issues are taking hold in a growing number of communities throughout the country. How is this possible? Because over the course of the last decade a surprising number of leading national religious and educational groups have moved from battleground to common ground on most school centered conflicts concerning religion and values. Local districts are using these agreements to build consensus among their constituents for new policies and practices involving religion and religious liberty.

The full extent of this progress became evident in December 1999 when President Clinton directed the U.S. Department of Education to send comprehensive guidelines on religion to every public school in the nation. For the first time in our history, all schools received directives on permissible student religious expression, guidance for teachers on study about religion in the curriculum, legal ground rules for cooperative relationships between religious communities and public schools, and advice to parents on a range of issues involving religion and values in schools.

This mailing was remarkable not only because of its unprecedented size and scope, but also because it contained advice drafted by a broad coalition of many religious and educational groups from across the political and religious spectrum. And it provided a legal "safe harbor" (or at least the closest thing to it) for beleaguered school boards, administrators, and teachers.[1] The documents included in the mailing were not a "top-down" attempt to tell school districts what to do about religion; they were a civic framework of guiding principles that encouraged local communities to develop their own policies under the First Amendment.

Just weeks prior to the president's announcement, another major agreement was released on the place of the Bible in the curriculum, surely one of the oldest and most intractable of the religion-in-schools conflicts. Published by the National Bible Association and the First Amendment Center, *The Bible and Public Schools: A First Amendment Guide* was drafted by groups ranging from People for the American Way and the American Jewish Congress to the Christian Legal Society and the National Association of Evangelicals. In all, twenty religious and educational organizations joined together to provide legal and educational guidance on how to teach about the Bible in ways that are academic, balanced, and fair under the First Amendment.

To fully appreciate the significance of this "Bible guide," we need only recall our painful history. The fight over the Bible began almost as soon as the common schools opened their doors in the early nineteenth century. Catholics, Jews, and others protested against a curriculum that imposed Protestant interpretations of the Bible. More recently, challenges to the constitutionality of Bible courses have generated lawsuits in Florida and Mississippi and sparked bitter disputes in Georgia, Tennessee, and other states. Now, at long last, leaders representing both sides of the debate have joined together to help schools understand the appropriate, constitutional place of the Bible in public education.

These two developments capped more than ten years of persistent efforts by educators and advocates (from all sides) to build a new consensus on religious liberty and religion in public education. The result has been nothing less than a quiet revolution that has begun to change the place of religion in public schools—a shift in thinking and practice that has broad implications for how we understand the role of religion in public life.

Two Failed Models

Finding common ground on religion in public schools requires everyone at the table to move beyond the two failed models that characterize much of the history of religion in the public schools and that still exist (in varying degrees) in many school districts.[2]

The first is what might be called the model of the "sacred public school" in which school practices favor one religion (historically, generalized Protestant Christianity). Found in public schools during much of the nineteenth century, this model survived into the twentieth century as a remnant of a vanishing Protestant hegemony.

The struggle to preserve the sacred public school continues to fuel conflict in many school districts, especially in the rural South. Until Lisa Herdahl won her lawsuit in 1996 (to cite one high-profile example), the schools in Pontotoc County, Mississippi, had prayers over the intercom and Bible classes that looked more like Sunday school instruction.

The second model is that of the "naked public school," based on what President Clinton has criticized as the mistaken idea that public schools should be "religion-free zones." Contrary to popular opinion, the naked public school is not a creation of the U.S. Supreme Court. While it's true that the Court struck down teacher led prayer, devotional Bible reading, and other "state sponsored" religious practices in the early 1960s, the Court has never told students that they can't say grace before lunch or bring their Bibles to school or share their faith with classmates. Moreover, the Court has gone out of its way to emphasize that teaching *about* religion—as distinguished from religious indoctrination—may be included in the public school curriculum. (This distinction works in practice only after sufficient teacher preparation and sound, scholarly resources are in place.)

More than the decisions themselves, the political battles surrounding the Court's rulings foster the view held by some Americans that religion has no place in a public school. Caught in the middle of shouting matches about God being "kicked out" or "promoted" in public schools, many administrators and teachers remain confused about just what is and isn't permissible under the First Amendment. Over the past four decades, horror stories of educators prohibiting student religious expression have helped to create, fairly or unfairly, the widespread perception among religious conservatives that most public schools are hostile to religion. Confusion coupled with fear of controversy also explains why religion has been absent from most textbooks and curricular frameworks until very recently.[3]

Of course, both the naked and the sacred public school are unjust and, in most respects, unconstitutional. And neither model takes religious liberty or religion seriously. Ignoring religion (or treating religious expression with hostility) alienates many parents, impoverishes the curriculum, and makes a mockery of the First Amendment. Imposing religion violates the conscience of many students and parents, disregards the First Amendment, and does nothing to advance the interest of authentic religious expression in schools.

Despite the weaknesses and failures of both models, the polarized public debates over "prayer in schools," sex education, the December dilemma, and similar issues reinforce the notion that Americans must choose between imposing religion in schools or keeping it out altogether.

The Civil Public School

In the late 1980s, a third model—what might be called the "civil public school"—began to emerge as the result of a growing consensus on the constitutional and educational role of religion in public education. This third option had gained so much support by the end of the century that the Clinton administration felt emboldened to recommend it to every school.

The core of the consensus about the civil public school is captured best in *Religious Liberty, Public Education, and the Future of American Democracy*, a statement of principles first released in 1995 by twenty-four major religious and educational organizations. Principle IV defines the shared vision for religious liberty that undergirds the agreement:

Public schools may not inculcate nor inhibit religion. They must be places where religion and religious conviction are treated with fairness and respect.

Public schools uphold the First Amendment when they protect the religious liberty rights of students of all faiths or none. Schools demonstrate fairness when they ensure that the curriculum includes study *about* religion, where appropriate, as an important part of a complete education.[4]

These four sentences do little more than restate the civic framework of the First Amendment's religious liberty clauses—our shared commitment to "no establishment" and "free exercise." But they do so in a way that captures the spirit of the First Amendment in practice: by describing what schools might look like if we actually lived up to the promise of religious liberty. Rather than telling public schools what they may not do, the statement opens the schoolhouse door to student religious expression while simultaneously keeping government out of the religion business.

The statement of principles is extraordinary not only for what it says, but also for who says it. In what is surely a first, both the Christian Coalition *and* People for the American Way are on the list. The Christian Educators Association International is listed, but so are the National Education Association and the American Federation of Teachers. The National Association of Evangelicals, the Catholic League for Religious and Civil Rights, the Anti-Defamation League, and the Council on Islamic Education join with the American Association of School Administrators, the National PTA, and the National School Boards Association to endorse the statement.

The list of sponsors suggests that more agreement exists than is generally acknowledged or understood concerning the relationship of religion to public schools (and to government in general) under the establishment clause of the First Amendment. At the heart of this consensus is the idea that public school officials should be *neutral* in matters of religion.

But what does "neutrality" mean? I would argue that ever since *Everson v. Board of Education* in 1947, the Supreme Court has taken neutrality as its touchstone in adjudicating establishment clause cases involving public education. As government institutions, public schools must be religiously neutral in two senses. They must be neutral *among religions* (they can't promote one religion over another) *and* they must be neutral *between religion and nonreligion* (they can't promote religion generally over nonreligion).

What is not often appreciated is the fact that neutrality goes both ways. Just as public schools can't promote religion, neither can they inhibit or denigrate religion. The courts have also been clear about this—but, of course, here is where the conceptual waters become muddy. What counts as inhibiting or denigrating religion?

The signers of the statement of principles would doubtless disagree on whether or not avoiding religion—in the curriculum, for example—rises to the level of inhibiting religion under the First Amendment. Some might argue that it is not constitutionally *neutral* for public schools to ignore religion. For many religious Americans, being left out is hardly neutral or just. Others would contend that while ignoring religion may be poor education (and bad public policy), it is not unconstitutional.

But all endorsers of the statement of principles *do* agree that ignoring religion sends a message (whether intentionally or not) of hostility toward religion. They unanimously agree that including religion in the curriculum is constitutionally permissible and educationally wise. And they fully endorse the idea that public schools must actively guard the religious liberty rights of all students.

Of course, a statement about fairness and respect—however lofty and inspiring—means little unless it translates into agreement on specific policies and practices that can be adopted in local schools. But before taking a closer look at if (and how) the vision works, something must be said about the legal and civic foundation that supports this "new consensus."

A New Legal Consensus

The decade-long movement toward common ground in schools was initially sparked by a "textbook trial" in Alabama in the mid-1980s. In *Smith v. Board of School Commissioners of Mobile County,* federal Judge Brevard Hand ordered the removal of history and home economics textbooks from Alabama public schools because they unconstitutionally promoted the religion of "secular humanism." In support of his ruling, the judge cited the virtual silence about traditional religions in the American history texts. He also argued that the values clarification exercises in the home economics books taught moral relativism in contradiction to theistic religion.[5]

Judge Hand was quickly overruled by the Court of Appeals for the Eleventh Circuit, and his decision was widely mocked in the media. But some educators and advocates of the First Amendment recognized that the trial had uncovered a serious problem. One didn't have to agree that the textbooks were unconstitutional to be disturbed by the fact that the public school curriculum largely ignored religious ways of understanding the world (while including worldviews that are antithetical to many religious teachings). Surely that wasn't fair. Public schools could—and should—do better.

The educational message of the Alabama trial (and a simultaneous textbook fight in Tennessee)[6] was supported by several textbook studies that also appeared in the mid-1980s. Although the two reports differed somewhat in methodology and tone, the liberal People for the American Way reached much the same conclusion as the conservative Paul Vitz: public school texts include little or nothing about religion.[7]

The trials and studies prompted a diverse group of educational and religious organizations to seek agreement on how public schools should deal with religion in the curriculum.[8] After a year and a half of intense negotiations and countless drafts, seventeen organizations, including such unlikely bedfellows as the Christian Legal Society and Americans United for Separation of Church and State, endorsed "Religion and the Public School Curriculum: Questions and Answers" in 1988. For the first time, a broad coalition of national groups stated clearly and unequivocally the constitutional and educational importance of teaching about religion in public schools.

Because religion plays a significant role in history and society, study about religion is essential to understanding both the nation and the world. Omission of facts about religion can give students the false impression that the religious life of humankind is insignificant or unimportant. Failure to understand even the basic symbols, practices and concepts of the various religions makes much of history, literature, art and contemporary life unintelligible.[9]

Buoyed by their success, the coalition pushed forward and produced two more equally important "question and answer" statements: "Religious Holidays in Public Schools" and "Equal Access and the Public Schools."[10]

At first, the idea of seeking consensus on religious holidays—especially with regard to the so-called December dilemma—was resisted by some members of the coalition. "Don't bother to call a meeting," said one Jewish representative. "We'll never agree on this issue." But after four months of negotiations, agreement was reached.

The process worked because all of the participants came to the table prepared to work for common ground. All were committed to civil debate, a commitment made possible in part because of the trust created in the first "Q and A" effort. And all agreed to take the state of the law under the First Amendment as the starting point for crafting a consensus about what schools may or may not do.

The breakthrough came when everyone around the table agreed that public schools should *not* sponsor devotional celebrations, but *should* teach about religious holidays. Jews, Christians, Muslims, and others agreed with educators that study about religion was not only the constitutional solution, but also the most authentic way for religion to be included in the curriculum. Remarkably, language was found to address Christmas, the perennial flashpoint in the religious holidays debate.[11]

A defining moment in the "religious holidays" discussion came just as the final draft was about to be adopted. A representative of an evangelical Christian organization spoke up to say that he wasn't satisfied. Why? Because, he said, "there's not enough language in here warning teachers not to use their position to proselytize students."

After a stunned silence, someone joked: "Don't you know who you're representing here?"

The evangelical lawyer didn't join in the general laughter. "Do you think," he replied, "that I want to impose my religion in the public schools?" (A few heads nodded almost imperceptibly.) "Well, I don't. Most of the people I represent don't want the government teaching our religion. We just want *fairness* for our faith in the public schools."

Another sentence was added to the document: "Teachers may not use the study of religious holidays as an opportunity to proselytize or to inject personal religious beliefs into the discussion." And the agreement was sealed.

The process of drafting the third Q and A, "Equal Access and the Public Schools," prompted another kind of lesson. Members of the drafting committee were deeply divided about the Equal Access Act passed by Congress in 1984. The act ensures that students in secondary public schools may form religious clubs if the school allows other "noncurriculum-related groups." The clubs must be student initiated and student led. Outsiders may not "direct, control, or regularly attend" student religious clubs, and teachers acting as monitors may be present at religious club meetings in a nonparticipatory capacity only.[12]

Some organizations involved in drafting the consensus guidelines believed that the act was unconstitutional (a view rejected by the Supreme Court in 1990) and bad public policy. Others hailed the act as the most important accommodation for religion in public schools in many decades. But around the table, both sides joined together to write the definitive guidelines for interpreting how the act works. The lesson: even strong disagreements on public policy do not preclude finding some common ground in service of the common good.

Since these documents began to circulate about ten years ago, thousands of copies have been distributed in school districts throughout the nation. The guidance they offer, supported as it is by a broad range of national groups, has been quoted and adapted in scores of state and local policy statements.

Perhaps the single most important step forward in the effort to articulate a legal consensus came in 1995 with the publication of "Religion in the Public Schools: A Joint Statement of Current Law." Endorsed by thirty-five religious and civil liberties groups, this agreement outlined the religious liberty rights of students and the constitutional role of school officials. That same year, President Clinton used the joint statement as the basis for a directive to all local superintendents on religious expression in public schools.[13]

The joint statement and the presidential directive were intended to correct the widespread misconception that student religious expression has no place in a public school. In fact, students do have the right to pray in a public school, alone or in groups, as long as the activity does not disrupt the school or infringe on the rights of others. Students have the right to share their faith with others and to read their scriptures. They may distribute religious literature in school, subject to reasonable time, place, and manner restrictions. And in secondary schools, students may form religious clubs if the school allows other extracurricular clubs.

The First Amendment Center has found that in school districts with religious liberty policies built on this consensus there are fewer conflicts and higher levels of trust among parents. Of course, some questions about how to apply the First Amendment in schools remain in dispute. For example, lower courts are currently divided about the limits school officials may place on student religious expression before a captive audience in the classroom or at a school sponsored event. But the legal agreement on many long-contested issues has begun to reverse the perception that public schools are (or should be) religion-free zones.

The process that produced these consensus statements reflects a public philosophy—however unspoken and half-conscious—that calls Americans to work together as citizens for the common good.

Guiding Principles for Civic Agreement

The success of these public school initiatives illustrates the vision and promise of the Williamsburg Charter: within clearly articulated constitutional principles, Americans with significant ideological and religious differences are able to forge agreement on the role

of religion in schools and in public life. Even more than legal agreements, the charter has proved to be the most significant and lasting
contribution to "common ground" efforts in public education.

At the heart of the charter is an agreement on democratic first
principles, a civic framework within which citizens are able to negotiate profound disagreements in the public square of America.
Os Guinness, who led in drafting the document, describes this principled agreement as "chartered pluralism." By this he means "a vision of religious liberty in public life that, across the deep religious
differences of a pluralistic society, guarantees and sustains religious
liberty for all by forging a substantive agreement, or freely chosen
compact, over three things that are the 'Three Rs' of religious liberty: rights, responsibilities, and respect."[14]

The summary of principles of the charter describes these "Three
Rs" in the following way:

[Rights] Religious liberty, freedom of conscience, is a precious, fundamental
and inalienable right. A society is only as just and free as it is respectful of this
right for its smallest minorities and least popular communities.

[Responsibilities] Rights are best guarded and responsibilities best exercised
when each person and group guards for all others those rights they wish
guarded for themselves.

[Respect] Conflict and debate are vital to democracy. Yet if controversies about
religion and politics are to reflect the highest wisdom of the First Amendment
and advance the best interests of the disputants and the nation, then *how* we
debate, and not only *what* we debate, is critical.[15]

The Williamsburg Charter makes clear that although a religious
consensus in our diverse nation is not possible, agreement on civic
principles is not only possible but also urgently needed. A principled compact that spells out the rights, responsibilities, and respect
required by our commitment to religious liberty creates a civic unity
that serves the interests of our religious diversity.

The Charter sets forth a renewed national compact, in the sense of a solemn
mutual agreement between parties, on how we view the place of religion in
American life and how we should contend with each other's deepest differences
in the public sphere. It is a call to a vision of public life that will allow conflict
to lead to consensus, religious commitment to reinforce political civility. In this
way, diversity is not a point of weakness but a source of strength.

Applying the Principles

In the early 1990s, drafters and supporters of the Williamsburg Charter launched a series of initiatives aimed at implementing in public schools the civic framework of the compact. By 1994 these efforts were housed at the Freedom Forum's First Amendment Center at Vanderbilt University. The goal was to use the emerging consensus on the law and the vision of the charter to encourage what I have called civil public schools: schools that model the First Amendment principles of "rights, responsibilities, and respect."

By the end of the century, there were two statewide "Three Rs" projects in California and Utah and many similar initiatives in local school districts throughout the nation. These projects are successful case studies showing how Americans can use civic principles as a framework for finding common ground. Supported by a broad cross-section of educational and religious organizations, Three Rs programs prepare teams of parents, community leaders, school board members, teachers, and administrators in local districts to understand and apply religious liberty principles. The programs also help teachers to teach about religions in ways that are constitutionally permissible and educationally sound.

The good news is that this approach works.

- Once the school board in Snowline—a southern California district near San Bernardino—adopted the Three Rs framework as their ground rules for addressing conflicts, they were able to resolve peacefully a series of disputes involving the curriculum. As a result, some homeschooling parents actually *returned* their children to the public schools.
- In Ramona, a district near San Diego, a Common Ground Task Force was formed to develop and implement religious liberty policies for the schools. Ramona now has a model policy on religion in schools and a successful process for finding solutions to disputes about religion and values.
- Davis County, Utah, recently passed a comprehensive policy on a wide range of religious liberty issues and has offered in-service training to implement it. Now parents are more supportive of the schools, administrators are clearer about the

constitutional ground rules, and teachers are becoming better prepared to deal with religion in the classroom.

These and similar efforts are successful because first, the key stakeholders—including the critics of the schools—are fully represented in the process of reaching agreement on civic principles, and second, the districts commit themselves to follow-through training and careful implementation. Schools in Wicomico County, Maryland, for example, made sure that the community was informed and involved at every stage. Through town meetings and the media, citizens knew what was going on and were able to participate in the discussion. When a policy on religion was adopted, it was widely disseminated, administrators were trained to use it, and teachers were involved in staff development focused on teaching about religion in the curriculum.

Of course, in all of these communities there are still "winners and losers" on policy issues involving religious differences. But if all sides are treated with fairness and respect, then those who lose one debate are more likely to continue working within the schools, especially if they win other battles. The key seems to be for school districts to develop an understanding of religious liberty principles that all sides accept as civic ground rules for resolving conflict.

Today, growing numbers of communities are translating the vision of the Williamsburg Charter into practical programs and policies for their schools. From northern California to Long Island, New York, Americans with deep religious and ideological differences have found a way to work together for the common good. As attorney Oliver Thomas—one of the leaders of this effort—points out: "We don't have a bad story yet."

The Challenges Ahead

In spite of some school districts' significant progress, many barriers and challenges remain before the "civil public school" becomes a reality in most of the nation. Moving from national agreements about the role of religion in public education to effective local policies isn't easy in places where litigation is the first recourse instead of the last.

On one side of the debate, the longing for public schools that formally acknowledge God in some fashion—the "sacred public school" model—remains strong in many areas of the nation. Consider the anger and resentment directed at Lisa Herdahl in Pontotoc County, Mississippi, after she challenged prayers over the school intercom in 1993, or the bitter lawsuit over Bible classes in Ft. Myers, Florida, in 1997, or the attempt in 1999 by a small school district in California to use Christian textbooks in the public schools.

On the other end of the spectrum, some school officials seem confused or even outright hostile about the place of religion in the schools. Recent examples include the Michigan superintendent who prohibited a student from distributing religious literature to classmates, the North Carolina teacher who told a Christian student that her creationist views were nonsense, and the California principal who prohibited a religious club from meeting during lunch even though other extracurricular clubs are permitted to do so.

Of all these fights, it is perhaps the case involving first-grader Zachary Hood that best illustrates the complex and painful process by which the need to guard religious freedom is balanced against the need to keep public schools from endorsing religion. No one disputes the basic facts. A first-grade teacher told her students that, as a reward for doing well in reading, they could read a story of their own choosing to the entire class. Zachary Hood chose to read a story from *The Beginners Bible* about Jacob reuniting with his brother Esau. The passage selected didn't mention God. Concerned that the other children might think that she was endorsing the Bible, the teacher didn't allow Zachary to read the story to the class. Instead, she asked him to read it to her privately. The child went home hurt and upset. After attempts by the parents to work things out with the teacher and principal failed, Zachary's family filed suit. A lower court sided with the school, ruling that the teacher had the authority to prevent Zachary from reading his story to the class. In September 2000 the 3rd Circuit Court of Appeals split 6-6 on the issue. Zachery's family is appealing to the U.S. Supreme Court.

This unfortunate case pits two important principles against each other. On one hand, we can surely agree that teachers of young children need to control what goes on in their classrooms. The U.S. Department of Education guidelines do advise that "students may express their beliefs about religion in the form of homework, artwork, and other written and oral assignments free of discrimination based on the religious content of their submissions." But this is qualified in the next sentence: "Such home and classroom work should be judged by ordinary academic standards of substance and relevance, and against other legitimate pedagogical concerns unidentified by the school." Thus far the courts have agreed with the teacher: the fact that Zachary's story was from the Bible was a sufficient "pedagogical concern" to prevent him from reading it aloud. "It is irrelevant," wrote the judge, "that the story had no overt religious theme; the speech was the book itself."

But on the other hand, students—even very young students—still have constitutional rights. While a public school classroom is not a public forum where students can say or read aloud whatever they choose, as long as a student is meeting the stated requirements of an assignment, the teacher shouldn't be able to arbitrarily censor the student's speech—at least not without a sound educational reason for doing so. If the story had been too violent or complex or in some other way inappropriate for a first-grade classroom, then the teacher's decision might make more sense. But Zachary was not giving a sermon or offering a prayer. A simple disclaimer by the teacher that "this is Zachary's favorite story" would have been sufficient to allay any concerns about "school endorsement" of religion.

This is the kind of high-profile lawsuit that convinces many parents that public schools are hostile to religion. I would argue that, by deferring to the judgment of school officials (a wise practice in most cases), the court in this instance has gone too far. It doesn't erode the authority of educators to insist that they have valid educational reasons for suppressing student speech. The risk, if any, associated with allowing Zachary to read his story is surely far less than the danger related to forbidding it. Allowing teachers to exclude Bible stories simply because they are from the Bible strikes many Americans as unfair and unjust. Moreover, such an action sends a message to children that there is something wrong or embarrassing about having religious faith.

As difficult as this and other legal battles are, they aren't the only—or even the greatest—obstacle to the task of creating the civil public school. The problem cuts deepest in the public school curriculum. Apart from superficial treatment of religion in some history and literature texts, the curriculum all but ignores religion. The conventional wisdom of public school educators appears to be that students can learn everything they need to know about all subjects without learning anything about religion (other than brief discussions in history and possibly literature).[16]

But surely this is wrong. Yes, the curriculum must be neutral concerning religion under the First Amendment. But it is hardly "neutral" (and certainly unfair) to leave religion out and thus implicitly convey the sense that religion is irrelevant in the search for truth.

In addition to the First Amendment argument, there are significant *educational* reasons for taking religion seriously. A broad education should expose students to the major ways in which humanity has attempted to make sense of the world—and some of those ways of understanding are religious. "Mentioning" religion isn't enough; we must find ways to acknowledge the importance and complexity of religious voices across the curriculum.

As I have already indicated, some progress has been made in recent years. But even with the prodding of the many consensus statements (and presidential guidelines) encouraging more study about religion in public schools, only small, incremental steps have been taken to include religion—mostly in world history. State standards are gradually beginning to acknowledge religion, most notably the California social studies standards adopted in 1998. And some history textbooks have expanded their treatment of religion beyond the "mentioning" that typified earlier editions. But these modest changes are far from a serious treatment of religion. Most of the current curriculum continues to marginalize religion in our intellectual and cultural life, implicitly conveying the sense that religion is irrelevant in the search for truth in the various domains of the curriculum.

Of course, many teachers know from experience that including substantive study of religion in the curriculum can be done, in spite of the poor treatment of religion in most textbooks and state frameworks. For years, Massachusetts teacher Jack Heidbrink has led in-depth study of religions in his world history classes. Near San Diego, Kim Plummer has handled many religious liberty issues in her diverse classes of middle school students and has managed to teach them a great deal about religion. And in Utah, Eric Holmes and Martha Ball have demonstrated that study about religion in elementary and middle schools is not only possible, but also vital for a good education. Religion is treated with fairness and respect each day in these and in many other classrooms—all without parental complaints or legal challenges.

To the extent that teachers do tackle religion, they are likely to do so in history or literature classes. But religions clearly have much to say about other subjects as well. Consider economics, a subject that many educators mistakenly think has little to do with religion. A review of the national economics standards and leading textbooks reveals that religious views of economic issues are entirely missing from both. As a result, economics courses in public schools say nothing about morality or religion.

Is this a "fair and neutral" account of economics? Of course not. As Warren Nord has pointed out, all religious traditions have much to say about such issues as poverty, consumerism, the environment, and work. But nowhere in the standards or texts is there any discussion of social justice, the view of work as a calling, the place of altruism and compassion in human life, or any other treatment of economic topics of importance to religious traditions. Most economics textbooks include chapters on Marxism and socialism. Why not a chapter on religious accounts of human nature, justice, and economics as well? Again, this isn't an argument for promoting religion or for indoctrinating students. This is an argument for including religion in the curricular discussion, for taking it seriously.[17]

Even though we might agree about the importance of study about religion, we have much to put in place before it can be done properly in public schools.[18] Teacher education will have to change dramatically for teachers to receive adequate preparation in the study of religion. Textbooks and supplementary materials that treat religious perspectives accurately and academically will need to be written. And, if religious studies electives are to be offered in greater numbers, certified teachers must be available to teach them.

Is all of this realistic? It's too soon to tell. But rethinking of the curriculum, though difficult, can be done. After all, not many years ago textbooks largely ignored the contributions of African-

Americans and women. That's now changed. The same reassessment must be undertaken concerning religion in the curriculum. If educators are to be neutral and fair under the First Amendment—and if they are to offer a truly broad education—then ways must be found to take religion seriously.

Clearly, enormous challenges remain before the "civil public school" becomes the universally accepted model for addressing religion in public education. Nevertheless, without minimizing these barriers and challenges, it is still fair to say that a shared vision for religious liberty in public schools—a vision that includes people of all faiths and none—is much closer to reality today than ever before in our history.[19]

Toward a Dialogue on Homosexuality

Consensus concerning the importance of study about religion, prayer around the flagpole, or Bible clubs is one thing; agreement on social issues about which we profoundly disagree is quite another. Just how effective is a civic framework or compact for "finding common ground" when the issue is as explosive and divisive as abortion or homosexuality?

A conflict that erupted in Modesto, California, in the late 1990s over the question of gays and lesbians in schools may provide at least the beginnings of an answer. The fight started when the superintendent of the Modesto schools responded to reports of "gay bashing" by asking the school board to include "sexual orientation" in the policy on safe schools. The board complied and adopted a document entitled "Principles of Tolerance, Respect and Dignity to Ensure a Safe School Environment."

Many religious conservatives in Modesto feared that the use of the word "tolerance" signaled that the public schools now "tolerated" homosexuality. (And that anyone who opposed the policy was, by definition, intolerant.) The perception that school officials were somehow endorsing homosexuality was reinforced when the superintendent sent a team of administrators to a workshop in San Francisco (!) on gay and lesbian issues.

Stunned by the protest, the school board invited interested citizens to join a committee that would be charged with "implementing" the policy. Not surprisingly, 115 people—teachers, administrators, parents, students, religious leaders, and other community members—signed up to serve. The divisions and distrust were so deep that the group couldn't agree on what the policy meant, much less how to implement it. After months of shouting past one another, committee members eventually invited a representative from the First Amendment Center to help break the deadlock.

Bringing someone in from the outside allowed all sides to take a step back and look at the dispute with fresh eyes. Rather than refight the battle over homosexuality, the committee agreed to spend a day focusing on the principles of "rights, responsibilities, and respect" that flow from the First Amendment.

After much discussion, the committee agreed that religious liberty or freedom of conscience is an inalienable right and that, therefore, claims of conscience (on all sides) must be taken very seriously. The group went on to agree that citizens have a civic responsibility to guard that right for others, including those with whom they disagree. Finally, they agreed to debate one another with civility and respect.

Once the group had clear civic ground rules, people were finally able to hear one another. Christian pastors discovered that school officials didn't intend to push acceptance of homosexuality by including sexual orientation in the tolerance policy. Nor did the school district mean to suggest that conservative religious people should be labeled as intolerant because of their religious convictions about homosexual behavior.

On the other side, gay students and parents of gay students discovered that the conservative Christians on the committee were not attempting to impose their religion, but rather to make sure that the schools were not taking sides on a social issue about which the community was divided.

The breakthrough came at the end of an especially long and difficult day. The group had begun to realize that everyone in the room had the same basic aim: safe schools for *all* students. A leader of the conservative Christians stood up in the back of the room to say that he was all for a policy that ensures safer schools. "We don't want anyone called names or beat up," he said. "After all, we're

Christians." That provoked a gay student (who was also the student representative to the school board) to stand up and say: "That's all I want out of this policy. I just want to be able to go to school without being harassed."

After that, this unwieldy and diverse committee was able to reach unanimous agreement on a "safe schools" policy. The words "sexual orientation" were still included, but they appeared within the context of every student's right to be free from intimidation, including verbal and physical abuse. Renamed "Principles of rights, responsibilities, and respect to ensure a safe school environment," the revised policy and a new plan for its implementation were accepted by the entire school board.

As painful as it was, this entire process established new levels of trust and understanding in the community. The same local pastors who had been most critical of the schools stood up in a public meeting to offer support to the administration. "I still don't agree with some of their decisions," said one, "but I now believe that they're trying to do the right thing—and that they'll listen to us."

For their part, Modesto school officials moved quickly to follow up the policy discussion with in-service training for administrators and teachers. Wisely, the district made sure that the training gave attention to religious liberty issues, including how religion was treated in the curriculum. And the district decided to build on the consensus about civic principles to articulate a shared vision for character education.

Much remains to be resolved as Modesto continues to negotiate deep differences over homosexuality and public policy. Nevertheless, the community has made a good start. As in the fall of 1999, when Christian conservative pastor Jerry Falwell met with openly gay minister Mel White in Lynchburg, Virginia, to discuss their differences, the Modesto community was able to identify a shared goal of reducing hate and violence. In both cases, agreement on the importance of civil dialogue and safe communities produced important, if modest, results. Falwell has toned done his rhetoric, and at least some gay leaders have demonstrated a better understanding of religious convictions that oppose homosexual behavior as a matter of conscience.

With issues as volatile as homosexuality, progress toward civil dialogue and agreement is measured in small steps. In Modesto, for example, as soon as the new policy was adopted, the goodwill generated was put to the test: what would happen if a group of high school students wanted to form a gay and lesbian club (a prospect that appeared imminent)? The district said it would follow the provisions of the Equal Access Act and allow the club, since other extracurricular clubs were permitted. But the school was careful to win support among conservatives for this decision by establishing a policy that would require *parental permission* to join any extracurricular club. When the gay club was eventually formed, the conservative Christian community continued to support the decision by school officials to keep the forum open. Such a compromise might well have prevented the shutdown of all extracurricular clubs by the school board in Salt Lake City a few years ago, or have avoided the refusal in late 1999 of an Orange County, California, school board to allow the "gay-straight alliance" to meet.

In both Modesto and Lynchburg, civil dialogue enabled all sides to find *some* common ground. At a minimum, agreement was reached to work for an end to hatred and violence toward gays and lesbians. Beyond that, both encounters focused attention on the importance of listening to one another as a basis for addressing future conflicts. In Modesto at least, gay and lesbian participants in the discussion began to understand more clearly why religious convictions made acceptance of homosexuality by most conservative Christians difficult, if not impossible. And conservative participants began to understand the pain and suffering of many gay and lesbian students. Both sides faced up to the deep differences that separated them—and then decided to do what they could to resolve the conflict *without* compromising deep convictions.

Taking the next steps will not be easy in Modesto or in other communities around the country struggling with conflicts over homosexuality.[20] Harassment and hate crimes directed at gay people in schools and communities often put the issue on the public agenda. But beyond general agreement about the need to promote safe schools and to work against harassment and hate in the broader community, Americans remain deeply divided about every public policy proposal concerning homosexuality, from gays in the military to same-sex marriage.

As societal acceptance of homosexuality continues to expand (as now appears likely), the question of how to protect religious conscience that opposes homosexual behavior will become more urgent for many conservative faith traditions. Legislation proposed in Congress to prohibit job discrimination based on sexual orientation exempts religious organizations (and does not apply to businesses with less than fifteen people). But as the rancorous debate over the Religious Liberty Protection Act in 1999 revealed, many liberal religious and civil rights groups are concerned that religious conservatives will use religious liberty claims to gain exemption from existing civil rights laws—especially those laws that include protections on the basis of sexual orientation.[21] Finding agreement on how to protect gays and lesbians from discrimination while simultaneously protecting religious claims of conscience will not be easy. Gay rights advocates would need to accept the need for religious exemptions—at least for small businesses and rental properties. And religious conservatives would need to accept the need for adding sexual orientation to the classifications of people protected from discrimination. On this and other public policy issues related to sexual orientation, there is an urgent need for serious and civil dialogue.

Seeking Common Ground in the Abortion Conflict

The other public policy and moral issue that most defies "finding common ground" is, of course, abortion. Not since the battle over the abolition of slavery have Americans been so deeply divided and expressed their differences with so much hostility, anger, and violence. The abolition debate helped ignite the bloodiest and most tragic chapter in our nation's history. Can we do better this time?[22]

For the founders of the Common Ground Network for Life and Choice, the answer is an emphatic "yes." Since 1992 this organization has worked to establish dialogue between pro-life and pro-choice advocates. Leaders and members involved in the effort include activists from both sides.

In striking contrast to the bitter and polarized public debate over abortion, the Network has created quiet but effective "common ground groups" in Cleveland, Denver, Dallas, Washington, D.C., and many other cities throughout the country. A key starting point is that no participant is asked to compromise his or her convictions about abortion. Rather than seeking agreement on the core issue, the dialogue focuses on building mutual understanding.

Honest dialogue is, of course, valuable in and of itself. But the Network pushes beyond talk to action. Participants engage in the difficult work of setting an agenda that people on both sides can support. In this process, most groups discover that they have shared goals concerning teenage pregnancy, the availability of adoption, the need for adequate day care, and other related issues. As a result, they are able to work together to change public policy in ways intended to reduce the number of abortions.

Will these common ground efforts succeed in recasting the abortion debate? That remains to be seen. But even the modest accomplishments thus far demonstrate that the Network is not a quixotic quest by a few idealists, but a practical exercise in civic responsibility with potential for broad support on all sides.

All Americans have a stake in the success of the Common Ground Network and similar initiatives. Charles Colson put it best when he warned (after the killing of an abortion doctor in Florida) that the crime "was not only senseless, it was symbolic—its message that a democracy poisoned by hatred and division can be as dangerous as the streets of Sarajevo. . . . Our public square threatens to become Matthew Arnold's darkling plain, where ignorant armies clash by night."[23]

Protecting Religious Liberty in the Workplace

Unlike public policy debates about abortion or homosexuality, there appears to be considerable agreement among religious and civil libertarian groups on the question of religious freedom in the workplace. In 1997 representatives from many diverse groups, ranging from the Southern Baptist Convention and the Christian Legal Society to the American Jewish Congress and People for the American Way, stood with President Clinton to endorse a presidential directive on religion in the federal workplace. The president acted in response to widespread confusion about when and how government employees may express their faith while at work.

Citing the principles of fairness quite similar to those articulated in the president's guidelines on student religious expression in public schools, the workplace directive makes clear that "neutrality" under the establishment clause does not mean hostility. The fact that the White House sees a need to remind supervisors that federal workers may read their scriptures during breaks or share their faith with coworkers is a sad indication of how widely "separation of church and state" is misunderstood and wrongly applied.

Evangelical Christians, Jewish leaders, civil libertarians, and others who participated in the drafting of these guidelines agree on equal treatment for religious expression, an interpretation of establishment clause neutrality that is of growing importance in Supreme Court decisions. Simply put, this means that religious expression will be treated in the same way as nonreligious expression. Of course, harassment and coercion are prohibited in matters concerning religion, as in other matters. But disagreement about religion doesn't in and of itself create a hostile environment.

The president's directive also specifies that federal agencies should accommodate religious exercise by an employee "unless such accommodation would impose an undue hardship on the conduct of the agency's operations." This would mean, for example, that a worker may have the day off for religious reasons as long as the absence doesn't make it impossible to carry out the functions of the department. Or that a worker who must wear a head covering for religious reasons should be allowed to do so as long as the covering doesn't interfere with the safe functioning of the workplace.

The successful agreement on federal guidelines led a similar coalition of religious and civil liberties groups to draft congressional legislation intended to protect religious expression in the private workplace. While the aim of Title VII of the 1964 Civil Rights Act was to require employers to accommodate the religious practices of their employees whenever possible, the courts have interpreted the act so narrowly that little protection remains for religious liberty.

In 1998 a bipartisan coalition led by Senators John Kerry (D-Mass.) and Dan Coats (R-Ind.) proposed an amendment to Title VII called the Workplace Religious Freedom Act (WRFA). Although the bill has yet to reach a vote, strong support from a broad range of religious and civil rights groups gives it a good chance of eventual passage.[24]

WRFA would require employers to make reasonable accommodation for an employee's religious observance, unless the accommodation would impose "undue hardship" on the employer. The key issue, of course, is the meaning of "undue hardship." The act defines the term much in the same way it is defined in the Americans with Disabilities Act. Thus undue hardship would involve imposing "significant difficulty or expense" on the employer. Such factors as the size of the business and operating costs would be taken into account.

In a nation founded on religious freedom, it is unfortunate that legislation is needed to get employers to accommodate claims of conscience. But in some places Muslim women are told to take off their scarves, Orthodox Jews and Seventh-day Adventists are told to work on Saturday, and Christians are told to come in on Good Friday and Christmas. In a recent survey conducted by the Tanenbaum Center of 675 workers (in a pool that included Christians, Muslims, Jews, Hindus, Buddhists, and Shintoists), two-thirds of all respondents viewed religious discrimination as an important issue in the workplace. One in five workers had either experienced religious discrimination personally or knew of a coworker who had.[25]

Since these are private employers and not the government, the free exercise clause of the First Amendment can't be directly invoked. But as the drafters of the Civil Rights Act understood, our commitment to religious liberty calls us to guard the right of each citizen to follow the "dictates of conscience" whenever possible. In this case, religious groups don't intend for WRFA to cause excessive hardship or expense for business owners. But they do want more flexibility in scheduling and more sensitivity to the religious requirements of workers.

The fact that coalitions from across the religious and political spectrum support religious freedom in the workplace may signal a new, shared understanding about religious expression in the public square. For most people of faith, religion is not (nor can it be) a purely private matter. Protecting and, when feasible, accommodating religious claims of conscience in the workplace or classroom uphold the spirit of the First Amendment and serve the common good.

Partnerships between Faith Based
Organizations and Government Programs

The coalition advocating religious freedom in the workplace (much like the coalition supporting the president's guidelines on religious expression in public schools) is bound together by a shared concern for protecting the "free exercise" of religion.[26] Much more difficult to negotiate, of course, are issues involving the separation of church and state, especially proposals that encourage partnerships between government and religion. Two debates in particular—one over the "charitable choice" provision of the 1996 federal Welfare Reform Act and the other over relationships between public schools and faith communities—have sparked sharp disagreement among religious communities as well as between religious and secular organizations. But as bipartisan support for both ideas has grown over the past few years, religious and civil libertarian groups have made a concerted effort to find some common ground.

Let's look first at the easier of the two issues: cooperation between public schools and faith communities. Given the enormous social problems and educational challenges faced by schools, it is hardly surprising that educators throughout the nation are reaching out to religious communities for help. What is striking is that these initiatives are strongly encouraged by the U.S. Department of Education and are spreading rapidly in large, urban school districts like Chicago and Philadelphia.

On this question, as with many others involving religion and schools, getting beyond the "naked" or "sacred" models of public education is a common hurdle for school leaders. Many administrators have studiously avoided dealing with religious communities out of fear of lawsuits and controversy. Others, especially in rural areas, have traditionally seen no problem with letting the local church send "Bible ladies" to teach a (unconstitutional) Bible course or with giving local clergy unfettered access to students during the school day.

But the new movement to encourage partnerships is pushing for a third model in the spirit of the "civil public school" outlined earlier. In 1999 a coalition of fourteen religious and educational groups published First Amendment guidelines for cooperative arrangements between public schools and faith communities. Lead drafters included the American Jewish Congress and the Christian Legal Society. Cosigners ranged from the National PTA and the National School Boards Association to the Council on Islamic Education and the U.S. Catholic Conference.[27]

The new agreement outlines how schools and religious groups may cooperate in providing mentoring opportunities, extended day care, recreational activities, and similar programs without violating the establishment clause. For example, the partnerships must be open to all responsible community groups and not just to religious organizations, and care must be taken to ensure that cooperative programs aren't opportunities for proselytizing of students during the school affiliated program. These guidelines were included in the Clinton administration's mailing to all public schools, along with a U.S. Department of Education booklet "How Faith Communities Support Children's Learning in Public Schools" that describes successful partnerships between schools and religious organizations.

In spite of this consensus among many religious and educational groups, a number of separationist organizations warn that these legal guidelines are only as good as their implementation. They argue that it will be difficult, if not impossible, to monitor or enforce rules against proselytizing during the cooperative programs. Moreover, distributing guidelines to all public schools may open the door to all kinds of religious groups that have long sought a way to reach public school students.[28]

It should be noted, however, that separationists do not uniformly oppose partnerships between public schools and faith communities. Groups like the American Jewish Congress and the Baptist Joint Committee on Public Affairs take the position that such arrangements can be valuable—and, in any case, are now a widespread and growing phenomenon that must be addressed. They are convinced that while national distribution of First Amendment guidelines may carry some risk, the greater risk would be to offer no guidance.

But support for the guide from religious groups with strong separationist views of the First Amendment is only possible because the guidelines are silent on the issue of government funding (i.e., when, if ever, government money may be used to support faith based programs for public school children).[29] As might be expected, the funding issue is why separationists are more united in their opposition to the "charitable choice" section of the 1996 federal Welfare Reform Act. Under this provision, faith based organizations may compete for contracts or participate in voucher programs when states use private sector providers for delivering welfare services to the poor. Although the funds can't be used for religious purposes, they can be given directly to religious institutions (including houses of worship) to administer programs on behalf of the government.

The Baptist Joint Committee, Americans United, People for the American Way, and other strict separationists argue that charitable choice violates the establishment clause by allowing "pervasively sectarian" institutions to receive federal funding to administer social services. By contrast, many Catholic, evangelical, and some mainline Protestant groups see the provision as a welcome opportunity to expand their services to the poor through creative partnerships with government.[30]

Now that charitable choice is the law, some religious groups initially opposed to the idea—the National Council of Churches, for example—are seeking ways to implement it without violating the establishment clause. And the American Jewish Committee has convened a number of groups representing various perspectives on the issue to explore the possibility of a common ground set of guidelines.

Though no new breakthrough has been announced, Oliver Thomas points out that many groups on all sides of the charitable choice debate appear to agree on a number of key principles. First, they agree that there is a role for faith based programs in the delivery of social services. Even most separationists will agree that government funding may go to religiously affiliated programs (e.g., Church World Service, Catholic Charities) as opposed to pervasively sectarian institutions such as churches. Second, they agree that secular alternatives should be available for clients receiving services through religious institutions. Third, they don't believe that direct government funding should go toward explicitly religious activities such as worship. And fourth, they agree that services should not be denied to anyone on the basis of religious belief or nonbelief.

It may be difficult, if not impossible, to reach common ground on the issue of government funds going directly to local congregations. Many separationists are firmly convinced that charitable choice and similar proposals violate liberty of conscience by forcing taxpayers to support religious institutions and that no list of "safeguards" will be sufficient to prevent government money from being used to proselytize. Many evangelicals and others oppose attempts to impose conditions on funding that would require churches to eliminate the religious character or symbols from their programs for the poor.

One possibility for bridging this gap might be to require that workers delivering the services be hired on a nondiscriminatory basis, thus creating the probability of a religiously diverse workforce for the funded program. (The Department of Housing and Urban Development, for example, currently requires faith based providers "not to discriminate on the basis of religion in hiring.") Getting agreement on this requirement will be challenging, since it is not currently mandated by the Welfare Reform Act, and religious groups may be unwilling to waive their right to discriminate in hiring on the basis of religion under Title VII of the Civil Rights Act.

In spite of the barriers to reaching agreement, all sides—particularly the traditional separationists—have good reasons to keep trying. The sentiment in Congress and in many states is to expand opportunities for faith based organizations to deliver government funded social services. Barring a successful court challenge, government partnerships with faith based programs are likely to proliferate in the coming decade. Without sufficient safeguards, groups on all sides have cause to worry. Religious institutions may find their autonomy threatened by government monitoring and auditing. And Americans seeking government services may find themselves subject to religious indoctrination in violation of their First Amendment right to religious liberty.

Achieving consensus on whether or not charitable choice is constitutional—or even good public policy—is highly unlikely. But just as guidelines for implementing the Equal Access Act were successfully drafted and disseminated by groups with deep differences over the wisdom of "equal access," so *guidelines and safeguards* on charitable choice may be agreed to by a broad range of religious and civil libertarian groups. Such an agreement would not (and should not) end the debate. But it could do much to advance the common good by providing a principled framework for implementing charitable choice.

Toward a Common Vision
for the Common Good

In each of the examples explored in this chapter, the search for common ground is built on the conviction that the guiding principles of the First Amendment enable American citizens to work together for the common good across even our deepest religious and ideological differences. Will it be possible to expand and extend these initiatives as our public square grows increasingly diverse and crowded? If recent efforts are any guide, the answer is "yes"—but it will not be easy.

Here are nine proposals for "next steps" toward what the Williamsburg Charter calls "a shared understanding of the place of religion in public life."

1. **Religious liberty policies in every public school:** Religious, civil liberties, and educational groups should join together to encourage the adoption of religious liberty policies in every school district. The policies should protect the rights of students of all faiths and none, and should ensure that the curriculum includes study about religion as an important part of a complete education.

2. **Religious liberty education for every teacher and administrator:** School districts should provide staff development for teachers and administrators focused on understanding and applying the religious liberty principles of the First Amendment. Schools of education should ensure that prospective teachers and administrators are prepared to address religion and religious liberty. Teachers who will deal with religious issues should know something about the relationship of religion to their subject. Ideally, they should take at least one course in religious studies. To carry out these reforms, departments of religious studies in colleges and universities will need to cooperate with schools of education.

3. Standards for study about religion: State departments and boards of education should ensure that study about religion is addressed adequately in state standards. Religious studies should become a certifiable field, requiring at least an undergraduate minor.

4. Resources for teaching about religion: Textbook publishers and curriculum developers need to do more to meet the need for scholarly, age-appropriate materials for teaching about religion across the K-12 curriculum.

5. Sexual orientation, religion, and public policy: More dialogue is needed among religious and civil liberties groups on all sides of the debate about sexual orientation and public policy. An immediate aim might be to seek consensus on how public schools should address controversies concerning sexual orientation in personnel polices, student behavior, and the curriculum.

6. Seeking common ground on abortion: Religious and civil liberties groups on both sides of the abortion debate should actively encourage efforts like those of the Common Ground Network. Foundations need to provide substantial funding for expanding this dialogue in local communities throughout the nation.

7. Religious freedom in the workplace: Congress should pass the Workplace Religious Freedom Act and states should act to ensure the religious liberty rights of state employees.

8. Faith based programs and government funding: The American Jewish Committee has convened a working group seeking some common ground on charitable choice. Advocates on all sides of the debate should support this and similar efforts, and should work together to create consensus guidelines and safeguards for implementing initiatives involving faith based programs and government funding.

9. Media coverage of religion: Religious leaders and journalists should discuss how to encourage more informed, complete, and balanced coverage of religion in the media. Schools of journalism need to find new ways to educate present and future journalists about religious issues and perspectives.

Our national motto (or at least one of them) is *E Pluribus Unum*—out of many, one. But as noted historian Edwin Gaustad points out, we look around America today and see plenty of *"pluribus"* but very little *"unum."* That's why our urgent task must be to reaffirm the guiding principles that bind us together, the source of our unity as "We the People"—especially as found in the first sixteen words of the First Amendment.

As we have seen, when Americans do this by putting civic principles to work, we are able to debate our differences with civility and to create policies and practices that protect the conscience of citizens of all faiths and none. The Williamsburg Charter is right: only when Americans engage one another in ways that are principled and fair will conflict lead to consensus and religious diversity be a source of strength rather than a point of weakness.

Seeking this "common vision for the common good" is not an attempt to ignore or minimize differences that are abiding and deep, but rather a reaffirmation of what we share as American citizens across our differences. As Catholic theologian and public philosopher Father John Courtney Murray famously reminded us, the guiding principles that sustain the American experiment in liberty are not our "articles of faith," they are our "articles of peace." Now, more than at any time in the history of our republic, it is essential that we live and model these principles in our life together as citizens. Can we sustain history's boldest and most successful experiment in religious liberty and diversity? We must.

Notes

[1]For example, one of the documents included in the mailing, "A Teacher's Guide to Religion in the Public Schools," is endorsed by twenty-two religious and educational organizations including both major teachers' unions, five leading Jewish organizations, the Catholic League for Religious and Civil Rights, several evangelical Christian groups, the Council on Islamic Education, and the National PTA.

[2]The Williamsburg Charter suggests the image of a public school that is neither "sacred nor naked" but rather a "civil public school." Describing how the religious liberty clauses of the First Amendment work for each other, the charter states: "The result is neither a naked public square where all religion is excluded, nor a sacred public square with any religion established or semi-established. The result, rather, is a civil public square in which citizens of all religious faiths, or none,

engage one another in the continuing democratic discourse." Williamsburg Charter, June 25, 1988, reprinted in *Journal of Law and Religion* 8 (1990), p. 18.

³ A comprehensive discussion of how public school textbooks have treated religion may be found in Nord (1995).

⁴*Religious Liberty, Public Education, and the Future of American Democracy: A Statement of Principles* is published by the First Amendment Center at Vanderbilt University. (A full text of the statement is appended to this chapter.) I chaired a drafting process that included Ron Brandt of the Association for Supervision and Curriculum Development, Ernest Boyer of the Carnegie Foundation for the Advancement of Teaching, Steve McFarland of the Christian Legal Society, Elliot Mincberg of People for the American Way, and Forest Montgomery of the National Association of Evangelicals, among others.

⁵Nord (1995), pp. 160–198, includes an excellent discussion of the Alabama trial and the question of "secular humanism" in textbooks.

⁶*Mozert v. Hawkins County Board of Education.* For a full discussion of the drama surrounding this case and a balanced examination of the issues, see Bates (1993).

⁷Davis (1986); Vitz (1986); Charles C. Haynes, "Teaching about Religious Freedom in American Secondary Schools," (Silver Spring, Md.: Americans United Research Foundation, 1985). See also *Religion in the Curriculum,* a report published by the Association for Supervision and Curriculum Development in 1987.

⁸The drafting committees for "Religion in the Public School Curriculum," as well as subsequent agreements on "Religious Holidays in the Public Schools" and guidelines for interpreting the Equal Access Act, were co-chaired by Oliver Thomas, then legal counsel for the Baptist Joint Committee on Public Affairs, and myself, then associated with Americans United Research Foundation

⁹ The entire statement on religion in the curriculum is published in Haynes and Thomas (1994).

¹⁰Both of the statements may be found in Haynes and Thomas (1994).

¹¹ "Decisions about what to do in December should begin with the understanding that public schools may not sponsor religious devotions or celebrations; study about religious holidays does not extend to religious worship or practice. Does this mean that all seasonal activities must be banned from the schools? Probably not, and in any event, such an effort would be unrealistic. The resolution would seem to lie in devising holiday programs that serve an educational purpose for all students—programs that make no students feel excluded or identified with a religion not their own. Holiday concerts in December may appropriately include music related to Christmas and Hanukkah, but religious music should not dominate. Any dramatic productions should emphasize the cultural aspects of the holidays. Nativity pageants or plays portraying the Hanukkah miracle are not appropriate in the public school setting. In short, while recognizing the holiday season, none of the school activities in December should have the purpose, or effect, of promoting or inhibiting religion."

The statement reflects the coalition's attempt to stay within Supreme Court rulings on the meaning of the First Amendment's establishment clause. But it also recognizes that the law doesn't have all of the answers (especially in the murky area of religious holidays). Schools must think not only about what is legal or illegal, but also what is right and sensitive in a pluralistic society.

¹²A full text of the Equal Access Act and the consensus guidelines for interpreting the act may be found in Haynes and Thomas (1994), chapter 11.

¹³The drafting committee for "A Joint Statement of Current Law" was chaired

by Marc Stern of the American Jewish Congress and included representatives from the Christian Legal Society, People for the American Way, the ACLU, the American Muslim Council, the National Association of Evangelicals, and others.

[14]Guinness (1993), p. 250.

[15]Haynes and Thomas (1994), chapter 2, pp. 4–5.

[16]Nord and Haynes (1998) explore this problem at some length. The summary of the problem in this section is drawn from this study of the curriculum.

[17]Nord and Haynes (1998), pp. 105–114.

[18]A report issued on January 13, 2000, by the People for the American Way Foundation, "The Good Book Taught Wrong: 'Bible History' Classes in Florida's Public Schools," claims that all of the Bible electives in fourteen Florida school districts are being taught in ways that are unconstitutional.

[19]In addition to the new agreements on religious liberty in public schools, there is growing recognition across the religious and political spectrum that character education must be an essential part of the public school mission. The character education movement of the past decade focuses on core moral and civic virtues widely shared in our society, such as honesty, caring, respect, and responsibility. In response to the perceived relativism of the earlier "values clarification" programs, coalitions promoting character education (most notably the Character Education Partnership) are careful to emphasize the importance of local communities working with schools to identify the moral values they wish taught and modeled in their schools. Thus far, however, the character education movement has largely ignored religion. Of course, public schools must teach moral values without invoking religious authority. At the same time, however, character education should not implicitly convey the idea that religion is irrelevant to morality. Since character education often employs literature and history to convey moral messages, some of those stories and some of that history should make clear that people's moral convictions are often grounded in religious traditions.

[20]Some public schools have adopted materials or sent teachers to workshops sponsored by a number of organizations that promote positive images of homosexuals, including the Gay Lesbian Straight Education Network, based in New York City, and The Shared Heart, based in Lenox, Massachusetts. But most districts avoid addressing homosexuality because of the deep divisions in their communities.

[21]After the Religious Liberty Protection Act failed to pass, Congress enacted a more limited bill—the Religious Land Use and Institutionalized Persons Act—in September 2000. Both bills are examples of ongoing efforts by many religious groups to restore strong protection for "free exercise of religion" (seen by many religious groups as weakened by the Supreme Court in the 1990 case *Employment Division v. Smith*). The Court declared the first attempt—the Religious Freedom Restoration Act (RFRA) of 1993—unconstitutional in 1997.

[22]Hunter (1994) explores the possibilities for common ground in the abortion debate.

[23]*The Washington Post*, April 11, 1993.

[24]S. 1668, the Workplace Religious Freedom Act, was re-introduced in September 1999 by Senators John Kerry (D-MA) and Sam Brownback (R-KS). Richard Foltin, legislative director and general counsel for the American Jewish Committee, chairs the coalition of religious and civil liberties groups in support of WRFA.

[25]The Tanenbaum Center for Interreligious Understanding based in New York City released "Religious Discrimination in the Workplace" in December 1999.

[26]An earlier example of the shared commitment to "free exercise" was the coalition that supported the Religious Freedom Restoration Act of 1993. More than sixty groups, ranging from Concerned Women for America to People for the American Way, participated in the effort to restore the "compelling interest test" weakened by the Supreme Court in *Unemployment Division v. Smith* (1990). Oliver Thomas chaired the coalition.

[27]Marc Stern of the American Jewish Congress and Steve McFarland of the Christian Legal Society were the lead drafters of *Public Schools and Religious Communities: A First Amendment Guide.* The guide was published jointly by their two organizations and the First Amendment Center in July 1999.

[28]In response to these concerns, Secretary of Education Richard Riley added a "checklist" to the administration's mailing to all public schools in order to underline the legal parameters for cooperative arrangements between schools and faith communities.

[29]An early draft did, in fact, contain a section describing current law on the funding issue. But strong objections from a number of groups opposed to including any summary of this unsettled area of the law led to the elimination of that section.

[30]For the background and context of the "charitable choice" debate we are indebted to Melissa Rogers of the Baptist Joint Committee on Public Affairs and Oliver Thomas, formerly special counsel to the National Council of Churches—both of whom are participants in an effort by a broad range of religious groups to seek common ground on this issue. With a grant from the Pew Charitable Trusts, the American Jewish Committee, in partnership with the Feinstein Center of American History at Temple University, is conducting a two-year effort to find common ground on the role of religious institutions in providing social services under charitable choice provisions.

Religious Liberty, Public Education, and the Future of American Democracy:

A Statement of Principles

Sponsored jointly by:

American Association of School Administrators

American Center for Law and Justice

American Federation of Teachers

Anti-Defamation League

Association for Supervision and Curriculum Development

Carnegie Foundation for the Advancement of Teaching

Catholic League for Religious and Civil Rights

Central Conference of American Rabbis

Christian Coalition

Christian Educators Association International

Christian Legal Society

Citizens for Excellence in Education

Council on Islamic Education

First Amendment Center

National Association of Elementary School Principals

National Association of Evangelicals

National Association of Secondary School Principals

National Council of Churches

National Education Association

National Parent Teacher Association

National School Boards Association

People for the American Way

Phi Delta Kappa

Union of American Hebrew Congregations

Our nation urgently needs a reaffirmation of our shared commitment, as American citizens, to the guiding principles of the Religious Liberty clauses of the First Amendment to the Constitution. The rights and responsibilities of the Religious Liberty clauses provide the civic framework within which we are able to debate our differences, to understand one another, and to forge public policies that serve the common good in public education.

Today, many American communities are divided over educational philosophy, school reform, and the role of religion and values in our public schools. Conflict and debate are vital to democracy. Yet, if controversies about public education are to advance the best interests of the nation, then *how* we debate, and not only *what* we debate, is critical.

In the spirit of the First Amendment, we propose the following principles as civic ground rules for addressing conflicts in public education:

I. RELIGIOUS LIBERTY FOR ALL
Religious liberty is an inalienable right of every person.

As Americans, we all share the responsibility to guard that right for every citizen. The Constitution of the United States with its Bill of Rights provides a civic framework of rights and responsibilities that enables Americans to work together for the common good in public education.

II. THE MEANING OF CITIZENSHIP
Citizenship in a diverse society means living with our deepest differences and committing ourselves to work for public policies that are in the best interest of all individuals, families, communities and our nation.

The framers of our Constitution referred to this concept of moral responsibility as civic virtue.

III. PUBLIC SCHOOLS BELONG TO ALL CITIZENS
Public schools must model the democratic process and constitutional principles in the development of policies and curricula.

Policy decisions by officials or governing bodies should be made only after appropriate involvement of those affected by the decision and with due consideration for the rights of those holding dissenting views.

IV. RELIGIOUS LIBERTY AND PUBLIC SCHOOLS
Public schools may not inculcate nor inhibit religion. They must be places where religion and religious conviction are treated with fairness and respect.

Public schools uphold the First Amendment when they protect the religious liberty rights of students of all faiths or none. Schools demonstrate fairness when they ensure that the curriculum includes study *about* religion, where appropriate, as an important part of a complete education.

V. THE RELATIONSHIP BETWEEN PARENTS AND SCHOOLS FOR ALL
Parents are recognized as having the primary responsibility for the upbringing of their children, including education.

Parents who send their children to public schools delegate to public school educators some of the responsibility for their children's education. In so doing, parents acknowledge the crucial role of educators without abdicating their parental duty. Parents may also choose not to send their children to public schools and have their children educated at home or in private schools. However, private citizens, including business leaders and others, also have the right to expect public education to give students tools for living in a productive democratic society. All citizens must have a shared commitment to offer students the best possible education. Parents have a special responsibility to participate in the activity of their children's schools. Children and schools benefit greatly when parents and educators work closely together to shape school policies and practices and to ensure that public education supports the societal values of their community without undermining family values and convictions.

VI. CONDUCT OF PUBLIC DISPUTES
Civil debate, the cornerstone of a true democracy, is vital to the success of any effort to improve and reform America's public schools.

Personal attacks, name-calling, ridicule, and similar tactics destroy the fabric of our society and undermine the educational mission of our schools. Even when our differences are deep, all parties engaged in public disputes should treat one another with civility and respect, and should strive to be accurate and fair. Through constructive dialogue we have much to learn from one another.

This Statement of Principles is not an attempt to ignore or minimize differences that are important and abiding, but rather a reaffirmation of what we share as American citizens across our differences. Democratic citizenship does not require a compromise of our deepest convictions.

We invite all men and women of good will to join us in affirming these principles and putting them into action. The time has come for us to work together for academic excellence, fairness, and shared civic values in our nation's schools.

A World Safe for Diversity

Religious Liberty and the Rebuilding of the Public Philosophy

An Address to The American Assembly
by Os Guinness

Of all the countless stories of the incomparable wit and wisdom of Winston Churchill, there is only one I know in which he was bested in the repartee. As the account goes, he was in a London club one day, went up to a rather portly aristocrat, poked him playfully in the midriff and asked, "Is it a boy or is it a girl?"

"My dear chap," came the reply. "If it turns out to be a boy, I'll name him George after the King. And if it turns out to be a girl, I'll name her Mary after the Queen. But if it's just wind, I shall call it Winston!"

I begin with that story because the proposal I put forward for reforging America's public philosophy would unquestionably be considered windy nonsense to some people. I and others, on the other

OS GUINNESS is a senior fellow at The Trinity Forum. He has written and edited numerous volumes, including *The Call: Finding and Fulfilling the Central Purpose of Your Life* and the recently published *Time for Truth: Living Free in a World of Lies, Hype and Spin*. From 1986–89 Dr. Guinness was executive director of the Williamsburg Charter Foundation. In this position he helped to draft the Williamsburg Charter and co-authored the public school curriculum "Living with Our Deepest Differences."

hand, believe it to be urgent, timely, and practical. So I leave it to
you and to history to be the judge.

At the dawn of the twenty-first century, we not only look back
on the most murderous century in all human history, we look out
at the prospect of continued carnage and destruction. Rwanda,
Bosnia, Sudan, Sri Lanka, Kosovo, Chechnya, East Timor, Sierra
Leone, the Spice Islands—each is a stark reminder of the much-
heralded shift from "total war" to "tribal war" and the so-called
reprimitivization of human conflict around the globe.

Explanations abound for this dark harvest of prejudice, hatred,
and violence—ethnocentrism, fundamentalism, chauvinism,
racism, terrorism, and so on. But beyond any doubt it represents
a humanitarian nightmare, a witches' brew of ancient hatreds
in which tragedies such as war crimes, ethnic cleansing, mini-
holocaust, failed states, and genocide become recurring headlines
on the world's front pages. The cold war era of ideological conflict
has subsided, but far from ushering in a new era of peace, humanity is returning to an equally dangerous era of ethnic, racial, and
religious animosity. "Living with our deepest differences" is one of
the most urgent challenges of the modern world.

And what of the United States in its supreme moment of world
leadership? More diverse than its more homogeneous allies such as
Britain and France, yet more united than its more multiethnic allies such as Canada, America has always been the world's supreme
model of how to live with deep differences. *E pluribus unum* was not
just a motto but a stunning achievement. Addressing unity as well
as diversity, looking forward rather than backward, emphasizing
beliefs as opposed to belonging, aiming to be transformative rather
than preservative, America's "new man" was a remarkable blend
of unity and diversity, with both emphases together serving the
cause of liberty.

Today, however, the American contrast is neither so clear nor so
confident. From the culture-war controversies of the last thirty years
to the more radical expressions of multiculturalism, signs are that—
just as elsewhere in the world—diversity and division are more pro-
nounced in contemporary America than unity and harmony.
Needless to say, there is no moral or cultural equivalence between
America's controversies and the world's worst flashpoints. But more

is at stake than the loss of America's shining example. At a time when "living with our deepest differences" is one of the world's pressing challenges, any American faltering over this issue goes to the heart of America's deepest principles and proudest traditions.

Some of us, however, believe there is a way forward out of the impasse created by recent controversies—a way that does justice simultaneously to America's first principles; America's past achievements in blending liberty, diversity, and unity; and America's present realities of exploding pluralism that have stretched and broken traditional understandings of how to live with our deepest differences.

This vision of a reforged public philosophy was set out in 1988 in the Williamsburg Charter. The Williamsburg Charter was a bicentennial commemoration of the religious liberty clauses of the First Amendment to the Constitution that both celebrated a robust view of religious liberty and offered a framework for religious liberty in public life that made it free and fair for people of all faiths and none. Importantly, it was not a legal document but a freely chosen statement of civic agreement, which—if followed—would stop the dangerous drive to make everything a matter of law and litigation. In the years since then, that vision has been developed and applied in a series of Common Ground initiatives led (and described in chapter 3) by Dr. Charles Haynes of the Freedom Forum. Together, that vision of rebuilding the common vision for the common good and these initiatives, making the vision practical in the midst of America's current moral, legal, political, and educational flashpoints, address the crux of The American Assembly's present topic.

My task here is to set out a series of propositions that provide the framework for both the Williamsburg Charter and the Common Ground initiatives that have flowed from it. Although I was one of the primary drafters of the charter, these propositions are my own and do not necessarily speak for the other drafters and signers, or those who participated in subsequent initiatives. But that said, these propositions are offered as a foreign visitor's heartfelt tribute to the extraordinary first principles of the American experiment, and with the fervent wish that the United States in the twenty-first century will recover the brilliant prudence of its founding generation and continue to be a beacon of hope for free peoples everywhere.

1. Three Tasks of Establishing a Free Society

Any reading of the speeches and writings of the founding generation would underscore their awareness of the three essential tasks of establishing a free society. Stated simply, these tasks sound almost absurdly obvious. But a moment's thought also reveals that the second task is less understood than the first and the third far less than the first two—with significant consequences for today.

- **Winning Freedom:** The first task is to win freedom, in other words to rise up and throw off the forces of the tyranny opposed to freedom. This task, in its minimal sense of overthrowing an ancien regime, is clearly the work of revolution, which the Americans accomplished in 1776, the French in 1789, and the Russians in 1917. Almost too self-evident to need stressing, the task of winning freedom—while costly—is also the easiest and quickest of the three tasks.
- **Ordering Freedom:** The second task is to order freedom, in other words to secure the ethical and institutional framework in which freedom may thrive. This task, which the framers spoke of as "tempered liberty" and "ordered freedom," was supremely the work of the Constitution. And here, significantly, the French and Russians did not follow. In fact, because of their striking failure to ground their freedom philosophically as well as to order their freedom constitutionally, both the French and Russian revolutions spiraled down to demonic disorder, with reigns of terror that replaced one tyranny with another.
- **Sustaining Freedom:** The third task is to sustain freedom, in other words to perpetuate the liberties that have been won and ordered. In the passionate flush of revolution it is easy to overlook the longer-term dimensions of this third task. But to the credit of the American revolutionaries, they never lost sight of this challenge. From the prerevolution sermons of John Witherspoon to the Farewell Address of George Washington, sustaining freedom was never far from their minds. Asked what the Constitutional Convention had achieved, Benjamin Franklin replied typically, "A republic, Madame—if you can

keep it." Later, in the same vein, the twenty-eight year old Abraham Lincoln chose as his subject for his address at the Springfield Lyceum "the perpetuation of our political institutions." Far harder and longer than either winning or ordering freedom, sustaining freedom is the work of centuries and quite clearly the task that confronts us today.

2. Three Classical Menaces to Sustaining Freedom

A defining feature of the framers, and a stunning contrast with most contemporary Americans, was their deep awareness of the past. They were both revolutionary and rooted. To create a free society that would remain free, they had to use history in order to defy history. At the heart of what James Madison called this "new and more noble course" was a blunt realism about the reasons why previous republics had risen, prospered, and fallen. In particular, the most brilliant of the framers were well aware of the three menaces to sustaining freedom set out by such classical writers as Polybius and Cicero.

- **External menace:** The first possible "source of decay" (Polybius) was external. Suddenly and for reasons outside its control, a republic may be threatened by another power greater and stronger than its own. Such a threat can be monitored, but it cannot be predicted precisely. Besides, for obvious reasons, this menace will only rarely be America's principal challenge. Continent-sized, with a two-ocean buffer and astonishing human and natural resources, America is less likely to face this threat than a small city-state such as Athens or a tiny-island-world-power such as Britain.
- **Corruption of customs:** Polybius's second source of decay was through the corruption of customs. While the success or failure of a republic depends on "the form of its constitution," the constitution of a society includes not only its laws but its customs, beliefs, and traditions. If these are not guarded during a "high pitch of prosperity and undisputed power," the resulting "deterioration" will lead not only to a corruption of the customs but to a subversion of the constitution itself.

- **Passing of time:** The third classical menace to sustaining freedom is the passage of time, which Cicero laments as "the lapse of years," Edward Gibbon as "the injuries of time," and Lincoln as "the silent artillery of time." By this process the vibrant beliefs and ideals of one generation become "the antique manners" of another. In Rome's case, says Cicero, "We have retained the name of republic when we have long since lost the reality."

To be sure, the writers of antiquity were so weighed down by this "ordained decay and change" and its "inexorable course of nature" that they were pessimistic about sustaining freedom. The framers, by contrast, were optimistic. But Madison's "revolution which has no parallels in the annals of human society" was more than the product of eighteenth century optimism. It was based in the conviction that the American experiment embodied a practical answer to the three menaces outlined in the classical warnings.

3. Three Assumptions of a Constitutional Republic

Many contemporary Americans rest complacent about freedom beneath a double conviction that a strong Constitution is the sole necessary protection of freedom, and that the separation of powers is the sole necessary antidote to the corruption of customs. In short, many citizens have unwittingly moved from the moral, or constitutional, republic of the framers to the procedural republic of today. Certainly part of the originality of the framers lay in their refusal to entrust the survival of freedom to the care of virtue alone. But for them, giving no weight to virtue would be as rash as putting too much weight on virtue. The framers' position, commonly overlooked today, is much more balanced, emphasizing both the constitutional separation of powers and the indispensable role of faith and virtue in sustaining freedom.

Their position may be expressed as follows: while the framers knew well that religion could be disastrous for freedom, and that republicanism had earlier and elsewhere commonly been linked with irreligion, they believed that the self-government of the republic rests on the self-government of the citizens, and therefore that, rightly related, faith is indispensable to freedom. Their position, repeated endlessly, leads to a triangle of first principles with three interlocking points.

- **Liberty requires virtue:** Benjamin Franklin's well-known statement, "Only a virtuous people are capable of freedom," speaks for a rich theme in the framers' writings. It also accords with contemporary philosophers, such as Isaiah Berlin, who argue that freedom includes more than negative freedom ("freedom from"), it also includes positive freedom ("freedom for" or "freedom to be"). To this the framers added an untiring warning. If there is no virtue, neither the law nor Constitution can sustain freedom. As John Adams declared, "We have no government armed with powers capable of contending with human passions unbridled by morality and religion. Avarice, ambition, revenge, or gallantry would break the strongest cords of our Constitution as a whale goes through a net." Or as James Madison, the father of the Constitution himself, said, "Is there no virtue among us? If there be not, we are in a wretched situation. No theoretical checks—no form of government can render us secure. To suppose that any form of government will secure liberty or happiness without virtue in the people is a chimerical idea."
- **Virtue requires religion:** Once again Franklin spoke for many of the framers when he wrote, "If men are so wicked as we now see them with religion what would they be without it?" Such canny, semi-skeptical realism also underscores another point. Unquestionably the framers were not all people of orthodox faith. They represented a wide range of positions on faith, just as they represented a wide range of positions on the relationship of religion and public life. But without exception they believed that religion was essential to virtue. In George Washington's words, "Of all the dispositions and habits which lead to political prosperity, Religion and morality are indispensable supports."
- **Religion requires freedom:** Those inclined to be suspicious of the first two points usually are so because they view

them as a way to bootleg religion back into public life, perhaps even "imposed" in some establishment form. On the contrary, for here the framers were most daring and most original. As Madison argues passionately in his "Memorial and Remonstrance," the Christian faith does not need establishing, and ecclesiastical establishments are always disastrous for religion. Sometimes they erect "a spiritual tyranny on the ruins of Civil authority." Sometimes they have "been seen upholding the thrones of political tyranny." In contrast, he argues, "Religion or the duty which we owe to our Creator and the Manner of discharging it, can be directed only by reason and conviction, not by force or violence." Only a freely chosen, disestablished faith can ground the virtue that guarantees freedom.

4. Three Patterns of Church-State Relations

As the framers were well aware, the United States was the first great republic to be established since the fall of Rome. And nothing in its Constitution as the novus ordo seclorum ("new order of the ages") was more distinctive and daring than the first sixteen words of the First Amendment—the religious liberty clauses. Yet these two clauses also grow directly out of the formative experiences of American history. There are three main patterns of European church-state relations. Each came out of an event decisive for its nation and has cast a long shadow over subsequent generations—in America's case with strikingly beneficial results.

- **1789:** The first pattern is the French one, shaped by its revolution in 1789. The situation then could be described as a corrupt church allied with a corrupt state with the result that the revolution was a volcanic reaction against each. The revolutionaries' cry says it all: "We must strangle the last king with the guts of the last priest!" Religion, viewed as reactionary, went one way, whereas freedom, viewed as progressive, went another. French republicanism was therefore irreligious from the beginning, and much of France shows little change today.
- **1688:** The second pattern is the English one, shaped by the Glorious Revolution in 1688. Here again was an established

church, the Church of England, but even its harshest Protestant critics acknowledged that it was semireformed and allowed considerable room for dissent. There were therefore no volcanic reactions, no militant anticlericalism in reaction, and the church was allowed to fade away until it became the Gothic West Front of English national life, beautiful but innocuous and irrelevant.

- **1791:** The third pattern is the American one, shaped ever since the Puritan experience in seventeenth century New England but solidified by the First Amendment in 1791. Here there was no state church, so that in effect pluralism and dissent were established. But the result was that faith and freedom, or religious liberty and civil liberty, were closely tied. As Alexis de Tocqueville observed fifty years later, "In France I had always seen the spirit of religion and the spirit of freedom marching in opposite directions. But in America I found that they were intimately united and that they reigned in common over the same country." Not surprisingly, this brilliant construct was seen as a key part of the American way of sustaining freedom.

5. Three Legacies of the American Ordering of Religion and Public Life

The framers were hardly modest about their accomplishments in separating church and state. After the "torrents of blood spilt in the old world," as Madison put it, they had now found "the true remedy" for ordering religion and public life. As the Williamsburg Charter declares, "Thus, the government acts as a safeguard, but not the source, of freedom for faiths, whereas the churches and synagogues act as a source, but not the safeguard, of faiths for freedom." In short, religious liberty is far more than liberty for the religious. It is an essential part of American ordered liberty, with important national legacies.

- **Vitality:** Foundational to America's experience is the fact that the separation of church and state has never meant the separation of religion from public life but the fostering of a remarkable national vitality. Not so much despite disestablishment as because of it, the influence of diverse faiths on American society has become all the stronger for being indirect and unofficial. "Free exercise" in religion therefore precedes and parallels "free enterprise" in commerce. One is the child of disestablishment, the other of de-monopolization. Free enterprise makes it possible to compete freely in the marketplace but to do so in a "fair game" and on a "level playing field." Free exercise includes the right of a person or a group to compete freely in the world of ideas and to persuade others by the strength of arguments and the quality of lives.

- **Harmony:** The practical genius of the First Amendment lies in its ability to foster two things that elsewhere in the world have all too often contradicted each other—strong religious convictions and strong political civility. Parts of the world, for example Western Europe, are currently characterized by strong political civility over religious differences. But on closer inspection the civility is less impressive because the religious differences are weak to nonexistent in societies that are increasingly secular. In other parts of the world, for example the Middle East, religious convictions are so strong that not only civility but liberty and life itself are often overwhelmed. In contrast with both, most of American history (with some egregious but rare exceptions) is characterized by a blend of strong religious convictions with strong political civility that has fostered a remarkable national harmony.

- **Legitimacy:** With 75 percent of Americans in 1776 coming out of a Reformation background, there is no question that, historically speaking, rights were viewed as a gift of God, not the government. As Madison wrote, "A right toward men is a duty toward the Creator," a duty that is "precedent both in order of time and degree of obligation, to the claims of Civil Society." This grounding gave to rights both their legitimacy and their decisive authority. As Jefferson asked, "Can the liberties of a nation be thought secure when we have removed their only firm basis, a conviction in the minds of the people that these liberties are the gift of God?" John Adams, for one, worried about some future day when freedom would be undermined if national leaders came to believe that humans were "but fireflies" and the cosmos was "without a father"—a position close to much modern thought—but for most Americans in most generations the legitimacy of rights have been justified decisively by their freely chosen faiths.

6. Three Changes Altering the Traditional Understanding of the First Amendment

Change is at the heart of modern life, and open-endedness is the essence of what Washington called "the great experiment." It is therefore natural that the history of America is the story of the negotiating ongoing social changes within the framework of the framers' ordering of American society. This is certainly the case with the last generation and the constant controversies over religion and public life. Three changes in particular have called into question the traditional ordering of religion and public life.

- **Exploding pluralism:** Pluralism and religious liberty have been linked inextricably since the colonial days. On the one hand, religious liberty has made pluralism more likely. On the other hand, pluralism has made religious liberty more necessary. Thus the American story has always been one of steadily expanding pluralism—the Middle colonies in the eighteenth century were among the world's most religiously diverse regions. But for all the steady expansion since then, nothing rivals the explosion of pluralism in the last forty years that now includes members of almost all the world's religions and a marked increase of secularists—significant because so strong among the educated elites. With some school districts now serving nearly a hundred different religious communities, "whose prayer?" is a vital dimension of the controversies over school prayer.
- **Expanding statism:** "Church and state" have always been confusing terms in America because there is no single church, no single state, nor any clear distinction between the two. But even the better terms "religion and government" mask the extraordinary changes in their relationship over 200 years: What

has happened has been described as a complete "exchange of roles." In 1791 religion was powerful and central in most people's lives, whereas government was relatively distant and weak. Today the situation is reversed. Government is central and strong, religion relatively weak and marginal. Not surprisingly, the reverberations have touched religious liberty. The Williamsburg Charter states: "Less dramatic but also lethal to freedom and the chief menace to religious liberty today is the expanding power of government control over personal behavior and the institutions of society, when the government acts not so much in deliberate hostility to, but in reckless disregard of, communal belief and personal conscience."

• **Emergent separationism:** Beyond all question, disestablishment and the separation of church and state are at the heart of both the purpose and achievement of the First Amendment. On the one hand, they remove what in other lands has been a central source of hostility to religion—its established and often oppressive status. On the other hand, they disallow any religion from depending on state power, and so throw each one back on its own resources—thus fostering a climate of entrepreneurial freedom and competitiveness. But this traditional view of separation is a far cry from the "strict, total, absolute separationism" that has become prominent since 1947. Slowly, strict separationism has grown from a theory to a doctrine to an orthodoxy to a ruling myth. In the process the relationship between the two religious liberty clauses has changed. "No establishment" has become an end, not a means, and a new vision of church-state separation has become dominant—in which public life is inviolately secular and religious life is inviolately private.

7. Three Different Visions of the Public Square

The recent culture-warring over religion has been analyzed in various ways—progressives vs. conservatives, secularists vs. fundamentalists, strict separationists vs. accommodationists, religious "betrayers" (privatizing faith) vs. religious "bitter-enders" (dogmatizing faith), and so on. But behind the sound and fury of all the charges and countercharges, there are three competing visions of the public square. In light of the framers' vision for sustaining freedom, which one prevails will be of enormous importance.

- **A sacred public square:** Despite the disestablishment at the heart of the First Amendment, the United States long had an unofficial, semi-established religion in a preferential place in public life—Protestantism. As the nineteenth century experience makes clear, Protestants may have been oblivious to this situation, but Jews and Roman Catholics were not. One response to recent controversies has therefore been the attempt to re-impose an earlier state of affairs on present day realities and maintain a privileged position for the Christian faith in American public life. But in light of the recent explosion of pluralism, this solution is neither just nor workable. There are simply too many "others" for any faith to be given any preferential position in public life.

- **A naked public square:** The second competing vision is what has been described as a "naked public square" or "religion-free zone" in which there is an antiseptic cleansing of all religion from public life. The sources of this vision are diverse and not all secularist. To be sure, some citizens support this position because of their secularist philosophies. But others are religious believers who are strict separationists in constitutional interpretation, and many are simply people who recoil from seeing the endless conflicts. "A plague on both your houses" is the attitude, so the naked public square is the outcome reached by a different route. But however the naked public square is reached, the result is even less just and workable than the sacred public square. Not only does this vision favor a minority worldview even less representative of America than Protestantism, it represents a decisive repudiation of the historic American relationship of faiths and freedom, and therefore a lethal blow to sustaining freedom.

- **A civil public square:** The vision of the "civil public square" is that citizens of all faiths and none are free to enter and engage public life within the framework of constitutional first principles. As the Williamsburg Charter states, "The result is neither a naked public square where all religion is excluded, nor a sacred public square with any religion established or semi-established. The result, rather, is a civil public square in which citizens of all religious faiths, or none, engage one another in the continuing democratic discourse." What this vision entails practically is described elsewhere in this book (see chapter 3). I would stress only that it provides a constructive way forward because it goes back to the notion of covenantal, or federal, liberty that lies behind the Constitution itself. The present state of religious diversity does not permit agreement at the level of the theological origins of belief (where differences are often ultimate and irreducible). But an important, though limited, agreement is still possible at the level of the outworking of beliefs—if negotiated within a freely chosen compact over the "Three Rs" of religious liberty: rights, responsibilities, and respect.

8. Three Common Misunderstandings of the Public Philosophy

There are many obstacles in the way of reforging a civil public square—not least that many of the culture-warrior activists have a vested interest in continuing the culture wars. But beneath an understandable caution, if not skepticism, are three common misunderstandings of what is in mind.

- **Civil religion:** First used by Jean-Jacques Rousseau as part of his theory of social contract, "civil religion" has come to be used of a nation's faith in itself through which it expresses its self-awareness, cements its solidarity, celebrates its unity, and actually worships itself. It is therefore quite incongruous with Judaism and the Christian faith, both of which severely condemn idolatry, nationalistic or otherwise. In spite of this fact, however, it is clear that "Protestant-Catholic-Jew" has been at the heart of the rise of an American civil religion in the twentieth century. The reforged public philosophy must therefore be distinguished from civil religion. Civil religion is essentially religious, and therefore discriminatory to those who are not

religious as well as idolatrous to many who are. The reforged
public philosophy is not in itself religious. It provides a framework for both religious and nonreligious citizens to enter public
life, but the framework itself is the expression of constitutional
first principles, not religious beliefs.

- **Lowest-common-denominator ecumenism:** A second
  misunderstanding is that the public philosophy is achieved
  through dialogue in search of the common core of diverse religious beliefs. While strongly espoused in some circles, this
  approach has insuperable problems. For one thing, however ec-
  umenically inclusive, it still excludes the nonreligious who have
  no interest in what unites religious believers. For another, it
  holds out the promise of a core unity that is a mirage. For all
  the talk of a "common core" to world religions, no one has ever
  been able to agree what the common core is. Equally importantly, globalization and the dramatic awareness of cultural diversity are underscoring an important lesson: differences make
  a difference. Respect for human life and human rights, for instance, is quite simply not a matter of universal agreement.
  The "universal rights" of the United Nations' Charter are
  anything but. Many of the world's religions and ideologies
  have no basis for or interest in such rights. It is important to
  know what we prize as inalienable—and why.

- **Indifferentism:** The third common misunderstanding is
  that the public philosophy requires such a neutering of religious beliefs that the resulting civility is another word for in-
  offensiveness and indifference. To be sure, some forms of
  "tolerance" have led to indifference. Infinitely preferable to intolerance, tolerance can become so vacuous that it topples
  over into intolerance—when it disallows the particularities of
  beliefs. "Respect" is a stronger notion, but it too needs rescu-
  ing from confusion. There is a difference, for example, between the notion of "the right to believe anything" and the
  notion that "anything anyone believes is right." The former is
  freedom of conscience, the latter nonsense. Put differently,
  there are no constitutional limits to what a person may believe,
  but there are definite philosophical, moral, and sociological
  limits.

Certain things follow from this tough view of the civil public square. Religion in the civil public square is not a religion of civility. Nor is civility to be equated with niceness. In democratic debates there are always winners and losers. Disagreement itself is an achievement. Civility is neither for faint hearts nor weak faiths. It is a framework within which important differences can be debated and decided robustly and persuasively, but not coercively.

Can we rebuild such a public philosophy today? Is such a common vision of the common good the best way to "unite America's religions" (and secular worldviews)? Or is the search for a just and commonly acceptable solution as futile as squaring the circle or searching for esperanto? Clearly the way forward requires not only a sound vision but courageous leadership and the patient, costly application of the vision to the festering sore spots of our current controversies. Yet neither leadership nor courage of that kind is in plentiful supply in America today.

But if these eight considerations point in the right direction, American leaders cannot continue to treat religion in America as a nonissue or a nuisance factor. The religious issue is much more than a question of the rights of religious believers in modern society. Culture-warring over religion means that an essential part of American heritage is being called into question and with it the vitality and viability of the American republic itself. Both religion and religious liberty are fundamental to the Great Experiment itself as the framers devised it, and therefore to the future of liberty itself. Alexis de Tocqueville, a far greater foreign visitor to America, said of the two great revolutions of his time: "In a rebellion, as in a novel, the most difficult part to invent is the end."

Bibliography

Allen, Barbara. 2000. *Tocqueville on Covenant and the American Republic: Harmonizing Heaven and Earth.* Baltimore: Johns Hopkins University Press.

Baptists of Virginia 1699–1926, The. 1955. Richmond: The Virginia Baptist Board of Missions and Education.

Bates, Stephan. 1993. *Battleground: One Mother's Crusade, the Religious Right, and the Struggle for Control of our Classrooms.* New York: Poseidon Press.

Bernstein, Richard. 1983. *Beyond Objectivism and Relativism: Science, Hermeneutics, and Praxis.* Philadelphia: University of Pennsylvania Press.

Carter, Stephen. 1998. *The Dissent of the Governed: A Meditation on Law, Religion, and Loyalty.* Cambridge: Harvard University Press.

Davis, O.L. et al. 1986. *Looking at History: A Review of Major U.S. History Textbooks.* Washington, D.C.: People for the American Way.

Easterbrook, Gregg. 1998. *Beside Still Waters: Searching for Meaning in the Age of Doubt.* New York: William Morrow.

Guinness, Os. 1993. *The American Hour.* New York: The Free Press.

Haynes, Charles C., and Oliver Thomas. 1994. *Finding Common Ground: A First Amendment Guide to Religion in the Schools.* Nashville: First Amendment Center.

Hunter, James. 1994. *Before the Shooting Begins: Searching for Democracy in America's Culture War.* New York: The Free Press.

Kelly, George Armstrong. 1984. *Politics and Religious Consciousness in America.* New Brunswick: Transaction Press.

Kuhn, Thomas S. 1970. *The Structure of Scientific Revolution*. Chicago: University of Chicago Press.

Little, Lewis Payton. 1938. *Imprisoned Preachers and Religious Liberty in Virginia*. Lynchburg, VA: J.P. Bell Co.

Lloyd, Elisabeth A. 1996. "Science and Anti-Science," in Nelson and Nelson (1996).

Lovin, Robin. 1987. "Social Contract of Public Covenant?" in Robin Lovin, ed., *Religion and American Public Life*. New York: Paulist Press.

Marcuse, Herbert. 1966. *Eros and Civilization*. Boston: Beacon Press.

Mitchell, Lawrence. 1995. *Progressive Corporate Law*. Boulder: Westview Press.

Nelson, Lynn Hankinson, and Jack Nelson. eds. 1996. *Feminism, Science, and the Philosophy of Science*. Boston: Kluwer Academic Publishers.

Nord, Warren A. 1995. *Religion and American Education: Rethinking a National Dilemma*. Chapel Hill: University of North Carolina Press.

Nord, Warren A., and Charles C. Haynes. 1998. *Taking Religion Seriously across the Curriculum*. Alexandria, VA: Association for Supervision and Curriculum Development.

Rawls, John. 1993. *Political Liberalism*. New York: Columbia University Press.

Scheffler, Israel. 1967. *Science and Subjectivity*. Indianapolis: Bobbs-Merrill.

Thieman, Ronald F. 1996. *Religion in Public Life: A Dilemma for Democracy*. Washington, D.C.: Georgetown University Press.

Tocqueville, Alexis de. 1969. *Democracy in America*. trans. George Lawrence. New York: Harper and Row.

Toffler, Alvin, and Heidi Toffler. 1994. *Creating a New Civilization: The Politics of the Third Wave*. Atlanta: Turner Publishing, Inc.

Tuana, Nancy. 1996. "Revaluing Science: Starting from the Practices of Women," in Nelson and Nelson (1996).

Vitz, Paul. 1986. *Censorship: Evidence of Bias in Our Children's Textbooks*. Ann Arbor: Servant Publication.

Witte, John Jr. 2000. Religion and the American Constitutional Experiment. Boulder: Westview Press.

A Charge from the
Leadership Council

To: The participants in The American Assembly program on
        "Religion in Public Life," March 23–26, 2000

From: Martin Marty, chair of the Leadership Council and the
        Religion Assembly

Members of the Leadership Council met with the three co-directors and The American Assembly leadership to review the background book and to make recommendations concerning discussion questions that participants will use at Arden House. On the basis of our review and recommendations we would like to pass on to all participants some sense of what we hope will happen at this program.

One way to anticipate positive meetings is to picture what would make up a disappointing one. We have respect for what The American Assembly has set out to achieve and on many occasions has achieved during the half century of its existence. We are pleased to see that the Leadership Advisory Group—the overall advisory group for the *Uniting America* Series—has given such prominence to the themes associated with religion in its *Uniting America* sequence. Indeed, some of the participants in this religion Assembly have signed on to this strenuous and promising endeavor in part to help recognize The American Assembly's investment in and hope for this topic. We believe that the participant list is quite representative and its members are thoroughly competent to make a contribution.

So it would be disappointing were we to go home having seen this as another "interfaith" or somehow "ecumenical" meeting, valuable as such gatherings are in other contexts, whose members were asked to represent their faith communities and engage in argument, debate, dialogue, and negotiations as part of an effort to come to agreement about substantive religious themes: e.g., God or non-god, or this or that particular way of pursuing their vision of ultimate ends. While people of faith and those drawn to deal with issues of faith may speak in the context of their most profound and particular commitments, they are not for this Assembly charged to seek such substantive results.

Instead, we shall have achieved something worth passing on to the larger public in print and in subsequent regional Assemblies and briefing sessions if we have produced some sort of consensus on some means of achieving proper goals—and we will discuss what "proper" and "goals" might mean—in respect to the task of uniting America in the face of ever growing pluralism, particularities, and, yes, passion in respect to religion, faith, and spirituality. It is this aspect of our common life together that has been disruptive and often destructive and to which we are poised to give fresh attention. And if that attention results in contributions recognized as original and rich, we shall have achieved our purposes.

The Leadership Council was enriched by the fact that voices not always or formerly central to such planning discussions were present at the table. The old "Protestant-Catholic-Jew" framework that developed after World War II does not do justice to contemporary reality. Thus at our meeting, among those who interacted were a Native American, a Greek Orthodox believer, a Muslim, a Hispanic Catholic. They were not there because they were elected by their communities or to assure that we would be "politically correct" or amply "multicultural" and pocketed in subcommunities each of which made its own statement without reference to others and to the common good. Instead, these Leadership Council members, just as all the participants, are expected to speak out of their own experience and their own studies of their "peoples," faith communities, and the like, in relation to the topics at issue.

Let us illustrate by noting what a Native American contributor brought in this anticipatory give-and-take. Our first discussion session will take up fundamental "Background, Values, and Goals" issues. While it became clear that for most citizens, the given situation implies reception and positive regard for the U. S. Constitution, would it not be important for everyone, it was asked, if we kept in mind that not all citizens asked to be citizens, approved the Constitution, nor have benefited from it in all cases? Native peoples find their religious practices restricted by existing property arrangements and laws of the land. Using their instance, can we not get fresh light on what most often take for granted in respect to "nonestablishment" and "free exercise" clauses in the Constitution—and thus perhaps come up with fresh understandings for the majority who are more directly in the constitutional heritage? A Muslim voice also will ask for a rereading of the story of national origins—as the chapter by Azizah al-Hibri in the book makes clear.

So as we discuss what are currently shared values and, indeed, what we mean by "values," it will become clear that we will be going "back to beginnings" and behind them, not for formal history lessons but for critique, affirmation, and what some call "selective retrieval" of that First Amendment heritage that colors the topic, themes, and realities of "Religion in American Public Life." As you participate in this session, ask yourself what your experience, whether in a faith community, a religious public, or through research, has to offer for a fresh reading of our values and goals.

The second discussion session will find us talking about "Religion and Public Policy." Here we will focus on two larger sub-themes: one will use current debate over welfare, government funding, and cultures of belief or faith communities—as they occur in respect to what today politicians call "faith based" ventures or "charitable choice issues." Clearly, the terms of public debate on this are shifting, and we hope that participants, in their reach for consensus, can make contributions. The corollary to that has to do with education in public life. Leadership Council members brought light from several angles. A Jewish participant urges that we discuss the role of religious communities vis-à-vis public education itself, in a time when through "home schooling" and similar endeavors there is a retreat from commitment to it. A Native American voice asks us to keep in mind what the compulsory, often brutal uprooting of Indian children by public agencies who used schools to deprive them of a heritage and customs can tell about some current resistance by particular faith communities. We hope that there will be new inquiry about how school curricula, performances, and practices will reflect present realities and help us work toward *Uniting America*.

The third discussion session will also ask us to take up "Religion and Public Policy," but this time looking at issues where we face more "intractable and permanent differences," not in order to "solve" those issues or to seek and find consensus over them. That goal would be so unrealistic as to be called Utopian at best and foolish at worst. The people who gather at Arden House are not likely to hear others there "jump" from, say, a "pro-life" to a "pro-choice" camp on the abortion issue—though miracles do happen. Nor will there likely be conversions or shifts on other troubling issues that now divide America and its faith communities, issues such as homosexuality, euthanasia, the use of material resources, and the like. Instead we shall use some of these to see if we can come up with proposals through a consensus. These proposals might demonstrate anew how we can live together with mutual respect in spite of differences; how we can hear "the other;" how we can part while disagreeing—and still find ways to pursue the common good and see religion as in many ways an agent that works toward *Uniting America* in ways consistent with the faith commitments.

The fourth discussion session will be of the "where do we go from here" sort. We will inevitably talk about the role of media both in advancing or retarding the understanding of religion in public life, and the potential role in the future. We might propose instrumentalities through which in local communities there might be fresh approaches to "civil debate" and dialogue. We will also ask you to propose ways of advancing and perpetuating what we come up with in the consensus document. In all these ways, this March 2000 meeting can help assure that "religion," however we define it and describe it, will have its rightful place among the five themes The American Assembly is addressing in its *Uniting America* endeavor.

Final Report of the
Ninety-Sixth American Assembly

At the close of their discussions, the participants in the Ninety-Sixth American Assembly, on "Religion in Public Life," at Arden House, Harriman, New York, March 23–26, 2000, reviewed as a group the following statement. This statement represents general agreement; however, no one was asked to sign it. Furthermore, it should be understood that not everyone agreed with all of it.

We hold these truths to be self-evident, that all men are created equal, that they are endowed by their Creator with certain unalienable Rights, that among these are Life, Liberty and the pursuit of Happiness. . . . *The Declaration of Independence*

. . . no religious Test shall ever be required as a Qualification to any Office or public Trust under the United States. *Article VI, Clause 3, United States Constitution*

Congress shall make no law respecting an establishment of religion, or prohibiting the free exercise thereof. . . . *First Amendment to the United States Constitution*

Preamble

We, the participants in the Religion in Public Life American Assembly, in recognition of our religiously diverse American union, reaffirm the intrinsic worth and dignity of each human being and our commitment to the principle of religious freedom. These principles are embodied in our founding documents, the Declaration of Independence and the United States Constitution.

Our deliberations come at a propitious moment. The arrival of a new millennium concentrates our minds, inviting us to evaluate where we have been and where we seem to be going. Looking back, we acknowledge that the aspiration for religious freedom has been a powerful force in the founding and development of the American democratic experiment. We also acknowledge that the United States of America has been a religiously diverse society from its inception.

Looking at America today, we see a broad new range of religious communities that have become part of our society in the past several decades. Most of the world's religious traditions are now at home here. America's increasingly multi-religious reality challenges all of us to affirm anew the common covenants of our citizenship.

Unfortunately, both in the past and today, our diversity sometimes has become a source of division rather than a display of human religious possibilities within a common civic life. We frankly acknowledge, and we lament, the use and abuse of religion, whether historically or currently, to divide us from one another, to generate animosity between groups, and, in some cases, to suppress the very liberties on which this nation was founded. We honor the ways in which religious voices can enrich us all, even as religious pluralism presents enormous challenges to us as believers and nonbelievers, neighbors, and citizens.

Taking up these challenges, we offer the fruits of our deliberations on issues ranging from the current meaning and implication of our basic founding documents and their twin commitment to disestablishment and the free exercise of religion, to how we debate current "hot button" issues like faith based social services, religion in public schools, school vouchers, or abortion. It is our conviction that, as a society, we will not be able to engage these questions from a stance of civility and respect unless we listen to one another and learn to take seriously religious viewpoints and commitments different from our own.

Americans live in an era in which religion is extremely visible in public life. Yet, as a people, we are uncertain about appropriate public expression of religion. This Assembly believes that the way in which its participants engaged one another offers a model of constructive encounter, and we learned just how difficult it is to arrive at agreement and to note disagreement with respect. If we, as a society, fail to learn how to communicate in this constructive way, we will either drift off into indifference or disengage in anger. Either way, this would be a civic tragedy. This Assembly believes that fruitful engagement in America is possible; indeed, it is needed now more than ever, given the volatile issues before us.

A Civic Framework for Religion in Public Life

The religious liberty clauses of the First Amendment of the U.S. Constitution presuppose a right to freedom of conscience based upon the worth and dignity of each person. The assurance of the free exercise of religion and the prohibition of religious establishment provide a civic framework for religious conduct and expression in public life. The effectiveness of this civic framework entails both public and governmental affirmation of every person's freedom of conscience, the responsibility to protect that freedom, and respect and fairness in the debates concerning religion that are inevitable in a society of such remarkable religious diversity.

This Assembly is convinced that the resilience of this civic framework and the possibilities it affords for diverse and robust religious life require sustained attention from American society generally and religious communities specifically. All across the country many communities are finding common ground on some of the most divisive religious liberty issues of our day. Encouraged by their successes, this Assembly challenges both the society and its religions to take the specific steps recommended in this document toward sustaining our nation's "lively experiment" in responsible religious freedom.

Challenges for American Society

This Assembly recognizes that although the principles of religious liberty are at the foundation of our civic life together, they have not at any time in our history been fully and fairly applied to all Americans. We call for an expanded understanding of these fundamental principles, taking into consideration our diverse heritage, and we urge a concerted effort to apply fully and fairly these principles to all groups in the society as, for example, Native Americans.

Respect for differences is basic to recognizing and protecting the right to freedom of conscience. Our civic agreement affirms that respect for competing claims about religion does not necessarily reflect agreement with those claims. Rather, it affirms the right of individuals and faith communities to bring their beliefs into the arena of public discourse.

This Assembly affirms a conception of our civic framework in which our citizens accommodate distinctive religious practices in the public sphere, including religious dress, calendar, rites, and ceremonies. The practical application of religious freedom depends on fair and accurate representation of religious communities in the wider civic culture—in schools, museums, and the media.

Challenges for Religious Communities

The American civic compact does not simply protect the diversity of religious practices; it also challenges religious communities to participate in working for the common good. We challenge religious communities not simply to tolerate religious diversity, but to reflect on the ways in which such pluralism can contribute to our common civic life. We further challenge religious communities to reflect upon the contribution that religious traditions can make to our understanding of the American commitment to the rights, dignity, and worth of persons.

We call on representatives of religious traditions to share their wisdom about concerns crucial to the improvement of life in contemporary American society. Among these are social justice, family life, racial and ethnic reconciliation, care for the environment, and the relationship of individual and community.

We call on religious communities to engage in outreach education about their own faith with other faiths and the larger society in order to combat stereotypes, increase understanding, and invite cooperation on shared issues of civic concern. We should be cautious about attributing a single voice to other religious traditions since we are aware of different voices within our own.

Finally, we call on religious communities to speak up for one another. When the religious rights of one group are threatened, religious freedom is threatened for all.

Challenge to American Society and the Religious Communities within It

Although ignorance is not the source of all problems, it is the source of some, and it is incumbent upon public education institutions, the educational arms of religious communities, and other organizations where people gather for civic action to make concerted efforts at a more substantive education of American citizens concerning the basic beliefs and characteristic practices of the nation's religious groups.

Religious Voices in the Public Sphere

Our deep commitment to these principles leads us to emphasize the importance of vigorous religious involvement in public policy and civic life. Americans should recognize that they live in a country with strong and flexible institutions, and a remarkable capacity for living with—and sometimes resolving—intensely conflicting views without recourse to violence. Religious voices are a vital component of our national conversation, and should be heard in the public square. We reject the notion that religion is exclusively a private matter relegated to the homes and sacred meeting places of the faithful, primarily for two reasons. First, religious convictions of individuals cannot be severed from their daily lives. People of faith in business, law, medicine, education, and other sectors should not be required to divorce their faith from their professions. Second, many religious communities have a rich tradition of constructive social engagement, and our nation benefits from their work in such varied areas as social justice, civil rights, and ethics.

We encourage people of faith to foster the emergence of a new American generation, one that better comprehends the significance of the increasing religious pluralism in this nation, and its implications for advancing civic dialogue. This will require people of faith to seek to communicate with one another and Americans of no religious convictions in ways that enhance mutual understanding and respect for the civil liberties of everyone. Because of existing realities, the burden for this process falls primarily on members of religious groups that have met wide public acceptance in their communities to help build the connections with members of religious groups that have not yet been fully accepted and to ensure that they are not treated as strangers in their own land.

When religions admit past offenses in their relations with others, they contribute to the achievement of this goal. This requires taking seriously the testimony of less powerful religious groups regarding their experiences of oppression. Religious communities across the land should express clearly their commitment to forging a common ground that allows us to address important issues in the public arena.

Educating for Citizenship in a Religiously Diverse Society

The participants in this Assembly wish to highlight the central role of education in providing citizens with a shared understanding of the role of religion in American public life. We urge all schools—public and private—to address the urgent need for Americans to learn more about one another in our religious diversity, to engage differences with fairness and respect, and to learn to work together as American citizens for the common good.

The public schools belong to all Americans. As guardians of our constitutional principles, teachers and administrators have a special obligation and responsibility to protect the religious liberty rights of students of all faiths and none, and to ensure that religion and religious conviction are treated with fairness and respect.

In recent years, a new consensus has emerged across a broad spectrum of religious and educational groups about many of the issues concerning religious expression by students in the public schools. A summary of these agreements and guidelines was sent by the U.S. Department of Education to every principal in early 2000. Unless these guidelines are translated into effective local policies and practices, they will mean little. It is, therefore, both timely and necessary for Americans to take the following next steps:

- Every local school district should work with parents and community leaders to develop clear religious liberty policies on student religious expression that reflect the new consensus under current law.

- School leaders should provide teachers and administrators in-service education focused on First Amendment and other constitutional principles and legal guidelines for implementing religious liberty policies.
- Colleges and universities should take immediate steps to ensure that administrators and teachers are prepared to address issues concerning religious liberty and diversity in public schools.

In addition to the importance of protecting the religious liberty rights of students, this Assembly also believes that the education of America's youth should include teaching about religion. If students are to be properly educated and prepared for citizenship in a diverse society, they must know something about the important role that religion has played in history and culture and continues to play in shaping our world. In many public schools, religion is absent or significantly underrepresented in the curriculum, and this contributes to a lack of awareness among students about the religious traditions that form the lives of many of their fellow classmates. The aim of instruction about religion should be neither to inculcate nor denigrate religion, but rather to foster greater understanding of religions. Critical to any teaching about religion in the public schools should be inclusion and respect for a full range of religious and nonreligious voices, and a recognition of religious pluralism as a source of strength for American society and democracy. At the same time, public school educators should be sensitive to the fact that religious faith often involves conviction about ultimate truth, and that for many people religious worldviews are not relative or interchangeable.

This Assembly believes that age-appropriate study about religion should be a part of all public and private elementary, secondary, and university education. In the public school context, we recommend training for teachers and administrators in how they can integrate study about religion into the curriculum. Training should be a part of degree programs for teacher certification as well as continuing in-service education. We encourage study about religion, where it naturally arises, in history, literature, and social science courses, and the development of elective courses in religious studies. Several states have already embarked on promising efforts to integrate study about religion into their curriculum, and we call upon other state and local entities to join in their effort.

We also believe that religious liberty and diversity are best protected in a school culture that teaches and models core civic virtues and moral values. Of course, parents are the primary educators of moral character. Schools should work with parents and others in the community to ensure that widely held moral values such as honesty, caring, respect, and responsibility are reflected and taught in the mission and environment of the school. This can and must be done without either invoking religious authority or undermining the religious convictions of parents and students.

Public Policy Issues on Religion and Public Life

Religious Liberty

Given that the principles of free exercise and nonestablishment are the twin pillars of the American commitment to religious liberty, this Assembly is concerned that the U.S. Supreme Court's current free exercise jurisprudence does not sufficiently protect the ability of Americans to practice their faith. Under recent decisions, the Court leaves it to majority opinion, as expressed in legislative bodies, to accommodate religious practices where neutral laws of general applicability may restrict such practices. Increasingly, religious communities feel burdened by the Court's approach to these issues. While recognizing that legislatures have sometimes proven amenable to passing legislation to protect practices under these circumstances, we nonetheless believe that the Court ought to accord greater deference to individuals and communities acting out of their inalienable right of conscience. The religious freedom of unpopular religious groups, and the least powerful among us especially, is too sacrosanct to be left to decision making by the majority.

Religion in the Workplace

Multireligious America has posed new questions of the workplace. In the 1990s, the Equal Employment Opportunities Commission reported a significant rise in complaints of religious discrimination in the workplace, including failure to provide a reasonable accommodation of religious practice. Although the U.S. Constitution does not prevent private employers from instituting work rules that burden religious practice, this Assembly is convinced that freedom of religion in the workplace requires renewed legislative attention. The Guidelines on Religious Exercise and Religious Expression in the Federal Workplace may provide a starting point for wider civic attention to this matter.

Faith Based Social Services

A central public policy issue at the present time concerns the provision of public funds to religious or "faith based" organizations to carry out social service programs of one sort or another. For example, the "charitable choice" provision of the 1996 welfare reform legislation specifies that state governments cannot discriminate against religious groups when contracting for services to help move welfare recipients into the workforce, nor can they require such groups to give up their religious values when acting as social service providers. While taking no position on the specifics of that provision, or all of its premises, this Assembly generally supports the concept of cooperation between government and faith based organizations in the provision of social services. The religious character of their efforts often can be integral to their programs. At the same time, this Assembly acknowledges that taking public money imposes certain obligations on faith based providers. These include, among other things, both the mandated responsibility not to use government funds for proselytizing, worship activities, and the like, and an obligation to be publicly accountable regarding their administration of social programs. Without laying down specifics, we call upon lawmakers, religious communities, and others involved in social welfare policy to seek to devise a workable cooperative arrangement that assures the religious integrity of providers and of those receiving the services, establishes standards of accountability for their use of the public purse, and ensures the availability of secular alternatives to the services they offer.

These important issues offer examples of the ways public policy ought to accommodate religious practices and undertakings. The experiment by this Assembly to address seemingly intractable religion related issues—including school vouchers, abortion, same-sex marriage, and assisted suicide laws—did not produce consensus. We believe, however, that the discussion of these issues conducted within a context that promotes civility, mutual respect, and nonviolence offers a model for society at large that holds the most promise for achieving areas of agreement among powerfully held opposing views.

The Media

We believe it is imperative that the news media adequately and accurately convey the character and varieties of American religious experience. It is indisputable that the American media have devoted increased attention to religious subjects over the past decade. Religion, which for decades could not be found on prime-time network television, today enjoys a real presence there. Across the land, dozens of newspapers have created "faith and values" sections and hired new staff to produce them. Hardly a month goes by without a "religion cover" on a major news weekly.

The news media, however, too often neglect stories with religious dimensions that do not tell simple morality tales. Religious perspectives on science, technology, ethical questions, and the arts—just to name a few areas—rarely see the light of day in either print or broadcast media. In many cases, reporters find it hard to come to terms with the religious motivations of the people they write about. The result is a picture of the world that leaves out one of its crucial dimensions.

When religious controversies make the news, journalists all too often seek out the most extreme views and ignore the frequent efforts of people of faith to achieve peaceful resolution. A journalistic tendency to polarize an issue by sensationalism can be particularly distorting in the religious arena.

We recognize, at the same time, that religious people need a better understanding of how the media work. Religious leaders have a special responsibility to educate their communities to understand that the media are not, and should not be, in the business of representing religion simply as adherents would want it to be represented. In addition, religious leaders and other citizens with religious commitments and perspectives who want to make their views known should take the responsibility to enter the public arena by means such as letters to the editor and op-ed pieces, visits to editorial boards, and use of the Internet.

A Plan for Action

We began this document with a reaffirmation of our basic commitment to the fundamental principle of the inalienable rights of religious freedom based upon the worth and dignity of each human being. We have developed a civic framework, articulated a call for citizens with religious convictions to engage civic life under shared civil rules for that engagement, and raised a number of vital and contestable public policy issues.

How do we move forward in light of our commitments, our claims, and our concerns? This Assembly urges the following agenda of action in the conviction that the well-being of the American republic may hinge on how we deal with the many issues and concerns generated by religion in our public life. Although we did not seek unanimity, we came to substantial agreement on a number of vital issues for which there is no single solution or definitive resolution. There are, however, things that can and, we believe, should be done.

Recommendations on General Principles

- We call for a concerted effort to apply fully and fairly the principles of this report to all appropriate groups in our society.
- We encourage an expansive approach to the accommodation of distinctive religious practices in the public sphere, including religious dress, calendar, rites, and ceremonies.
- We call upon religious communities to engage in outreach education about their beliefs and rituals with other faith communities and the larger society with the aim of combating stereotypes, increasing understanding, and inviting cooperation on shared issues of civic concern.
- We encourage holding town meetings in communities and on the Internet on the role of religion in the public sphere and using such occasions to model a robust engagement run by

people of differing religious and nonreligious perspectives. We also note the significance of the Internet in providing new and valuable sites for interreligious encounter in web based town meetings.

• We encourage the development of a national dialogue on religion in public life to provide a visible public forum for the serious and respectful discussion of matters of public concern by people of diverse religious and nonreligious perspective.

Recommendations on Faith Based Social Services

• Religious communities, lawmakers, and others involved in social welfare policy should seek to devise a workable arrangement for cooperation between faith based organizations and government that assures the religious integrity of providers and beneficiaries of services, the legitimate need for providers to be accountable for their use of public funds, and adherence to the mandate not to use government money for proselytizing, worship activities, and the like.

Recommendations on Education

• Local school districts should work with parents and community leaders to articulate clear religious liberty policies for students and school personnel that reflect the new consensus under current law.

• School leaders should provide in-service opportunities for teachers and administrators focused on First Amendment principles and legal guidelines for implementing religious liberty policies.

• Colleges and universities should reform their curricula to ensure that administrators and teachers are prepared to address issues concerning religious liberty and diversity in public schools and to teach about religion in their respective subjects whenever appropriate.

• Responsible citizens should encourage teaching about the role of religion in American schools, public and private, from elementary through university.

- Local schools should develop character education plans in co-operation with parents and religious leaders together with teachers and school administrators in order to ensure that widely held moral values such as honesty, caring, respect, and responsibility are reflected and taught in the mission and environment of the school.
- Communities and school districts should seek common ground on religious liberty issues as illustrated by the Three Rs Projects ("Rights, Responsibility, and Respect") of the Freedom Forum First Amendment Center and by the BridgeBuilders program.

Participants in this Assembly had the rare opportunity to debate matters of deep concern and commitment over a three-day period. We commit ourselves to continue this process by encouraging the formation of small groups in our own communities to discuss and debate the principles and recommendations of this report and other materials on religion in public life. As well, a subcommittee of this Assembly will develop and disseminate a study guide to be made available to leaders of local dialogue groups. We also pledge ourselves to widespread dissemination of this report in our own communities and states, including use of the Internet. For example, given our focus on education, we will see to it that those responsible for public education, from state superintendents of schools down to our local school boards, receive copies of this report, and we will encourage them to respond. We will undertake efforts to correct stereotyped portrayals of people of faith wherever they surface by embodying in our own communities concrete examples of how people with strong religious convictions can meet and reason together.

In the spirit of the *Uniting America* series of The American Assembly, of which this religion Assembly is one program, we believe that the recommendations of this Assembly contribute to uniting America.

Conclusion

We live in an era marked by widespread mistrust of our basic institutions and characterized by a crisis of leadership in many spheres of American life. No single effort or report can solve these problems. That will be the work of engaged citizens over many years. However, there is much that can and should be done as we have shown. Policy makers may have the most visible and immediate responsibility for civic leadership. But the democratic wager is that each of us has a vocation of leadership and each of us is responsible for the well-being of all of us as a nation and a people. Our diverse communities of faith are a rich resource to our nation, reminding us that we can come to know a good in common that we cannot know alone. This Assembly's work together has reminded us that religious liberty is a bedrock value that animates our republic, undergirds our civic morality, and defines us as a people.

Participants
The Ninety-Sixth American Assembly

*JOANNA M. ADAMS
Senior Pastor
Trinity Presbyterian Church
Atlanta GA

***AZIZAH Y. AL-HIBRI
Professor of Law
The T.C. Williams School of
    Law
University of Richmond
Richmond VA

SHARIFA ALKHATEEB
Vice-President
The North American Council
    for Muslim Women
President
The Muslim Education
    Council
Great Falls VA

NANCY AMMERMAN
Professor of Sociology of
    Religion
Hartford Seminary
Hartford CT

HADLEY ARKES
Edward Ney Professor of
    Jurisprudence and
    American Institutions
Amherst College
Amherst MA

††MARTHA H. BALL
Project Director
Utah 3Rs
Butler Middle School,
Teacher of Social Studies
Salt Lake City UT

**MARCIA BEAUCHAMP
Religious Freedom
Program Coordinator
Freedom Forum First
  Amendment Center
San Francisco CA

**KATHLEEN BRADY
Assistant Professor of Law
The T.C. Williams School of
  Law
University of Richmond
Richmond VA

DON BROWNING
Alexander Campbell Professor
  of Ethics & Social Science
University of Chicago Divinity
  School
Chicago IL

LYNNE BUNDESEN
Religion Beliefs Category
  Manager
The Microsoft Network
Microsoft Corporation
Madison CT

MARK CHAVES
Associate Professor
Department of Sociology
University of Arizona
Tucson AZ

LEE CULLUM
Columnist
Dallas Morning News
Dallas TX

JOSEPH J. DEPONAI
Chaplain (Major), U.S. Army
Office of the Chaplain
US Military Academy
West Point NY

WILLIAM T. DEVLIN
President
Urban Family Council
Philadelphia PA/New York
  NY

††DIANA ECK
Professor of Comparative
  Religion & Indian Studies
Harvard University
Cambridge MA

WILMA ELLIS
Continental Counselor
Baha'is of the Americas
Alta Loma CA

***JEAN BETHKE
  ELSHTAIN
Laura Spelman Rockefeller
  Professor of Social and
  Political Ethics
University of Chicago,
  Divinity School
Chicago IL

RICHARD T. FOLTIN
Legislative Director and
  Counsel
American Jewish Committee
Washington DC

C. WELTON GADDY
Reverend
The Interfaith Alliance
and The Interfaith Alliance
   Foundation
Washington DC

ROBERT P. GEORGE
McCormick Professor of
   Jurisprudence
Department of Politics
Princeton University
Princeton NJ

†DAVID R. GERGEN
Professor of Public Service
John F. Kennedy School of
   Government
Harvard University
Commentator
The NewsHour with Jim Lehrer
Washington DC

MICHAEL GILLIGAN
Program Director for Theology
The Henry Luce Foundation,
   Inc.
New York NY

**W. CLARK GILPIN
Dean & Professor of the
   History of Christianity
The University of Chicago
   Divinity School
Chicago IL

**ROBERTO S. GOIZUETA
Professor
Department of Theology
Boston College
Boston MA

MARJORIE B. GREEN
Director of Educational Policy
   and Programs
Anti-Defamation League
Los Angeles CA

STEVEN K. GREEN
General Counsel & Director of
   Policy
Americans United for
   Separation of Church &
   State
Washington DC

RICHARD A. GROUNDS
Assistant Professor of
   Anthropology
University of Tulsa
Tulsa OK

†OS GUINNESS
Senior Fellow
The Trinity Forum
McLean VA

STANLEY S. HARAKAS
Archbishop Iakovos Professor,
   Emeritus
Holy Cross Greek Orthodox
   School of Theology
Brookline MA

DIANA L. HAYES
Associate Professor
Theology Department
Georgetown University
Washington DC

***CHARLES C. HAYNES
Senior Scholar
Religious Freedom Programs
Freedom Forum First
 Amendment Center
Arlington VA

*WAYNE JACOBSEN
President
BridgeBuilders
Oxnard CA

ABDELMONEIM M.
 KHATTAB
Imam Emeritus
The Islamic Center of Toledo
Islamic Center of Greater
 Toledo
Perrysburg OH

DIANE L. KNIPPERS
President
Institute on Religion and
 Democracy
Washington DC

SAMUEL BILLY KYLES
Reverend
Monumental Baptist Church
Memphis TN

RICHARD D. LAND
President
Ethics & Religious Liberty
 Commission
Nashville TN

††SHABBIR A. MANSURI
Founding Director
Council on Islamic Education
Fountain Valley CA

****MARTIN E. MARTY
Professor
University of Chicago
Chicago IL

††ELLIOT M. MINCBERG
Vice President & Legal &
 Education Policy Director
People for the American Way
Washington DC

FOREST MONTGOMERY
Counsel, Office for
 Governmental Affairs
National Association of
 Evangelicals
Washington DC

WARREN A. NORD
Director
Program in the Humanities
 and Human Values
University of North Carolina
 at Chapel Hill
Chapel Hill NC

DAVID NOVAK
J. Richard and Dorothy Shiff
 Chair of Jewish Studies
University of Toronto
Ontario, Toronto CANADA

††KIMBERLY A.
 PLUMMER
The Preuss School—UCSD
University of California, San
 Diego
San Diego CA

MUJAHID RAMADAN
Imam
American Muslim Council
North Las Vegas NV

GLORIA G. RODRIGUEZ
President & CEO
Avance Family Support and
    Education Programs
San Antonio TX

GEORGE RUPP
President
Columbia University
New York NY

††CHERYL SANDERS
Professor of Ethics
Howard University
Washington DC

WILLIAM L. SAUNDERS,
    JR.
Human Rights Counsel &
    Senior Fellow for Human
    Life Studies
Family Research Council
Washington DC

STEVEN A. SCHAICK
Chaplain, Major
U.S. Airforce Academy
Center for Character
    Development
USAFA CO

*MARK SILK
Director
Center for the Study of
    Religion in Public Life
Trinity College
Hartford CT

HARRY S. STOUT
Jonathan Edwards Professor of
    American Christianity
Yale University
New Haven CT

††INES TALAMANTEZ
Professor of Native American
    Religious Studies and
    Philosophies
Religious Studies Department,
    HSSB
University of California, Santa
    Barbara
Santa Barbara CA

KENNETH TANAKA
Professor
Institute of Buddhist Studies
Graduate Theological Union
Berkeley CA

JOHN M. TEMPLETON, JR.
President
John Templeton Foundation
Radnor PA

††FORREST L. TURPEN
Executive Director
Christian Educators
    Association International
Pasadena CA

NICHOLAS A. ULANOV
Managing Director
The Ulanov Partnership
Princeton NJ

KENNETH WOODWARD
Religion Editor
Newsweek
New York NY

*Discussion Leader
**Rapporteur
***Co-director

****Chair
†Addressed this Assembly
††Panelist

Religion Assembly Leadership Council

Chair:
Martin Marty   Professor, University of
                                    Chicago

Co-Directors:
Jean Bethke Elshtain   University of Chicago Divinity
                                    School

Charles Haynes   Freedom Forum, First
                                    Amendment Center

Azizah al-Hibri   Professor, University of
                                    Richmond Law School

Leadership Council:
Joan Brown Campbell   General Secretary, National
                                    Council of Churches of Christ

Robert Franklin   President, Interdenominational
                                    Theological Center

Francis Cardinal George   Archbishop of Chicago
Roberto Goizueta   Professor, Boston
                                    College/Department of
                                    Theology

Rabbi Irving Greenberg   CLAL—Jewish Life Network

Os Guinness	President, Trinity Forum
Rev. Stanley Harakas	Eastern Orthodox
Mark O. Hatfield	Former U.S. Senator
Father Ted Hesburgh	Former President, University of Notre Dame
Iman Wallace Deen Mohammed	Ministry of WD Mohammed
Seyyed Hossein Nasr	Professor of Islamic Studies, George Washington University
Rabbi David Saperstein	Religious Action Center for Reformed Judaism
Kenneth Tanaka	Professor, Institute for Buddhist Studies
George E. "Tink" Tinker	Professor of American Indian Cultures and Religious Traditions, Iliff School of Theology

Uniting America
Leadership Advisory Group
(in formation)

Co-Chairs

David R. Gergen   JFK School of Government, Harvard; *The NewsHour with Jim Lehrer*

Karen Elliott House   President, International, Dow Jones & Company, Inc., *WSJ*

Donald F. McHenry   Georgetown University; Former U.S. Ambassador to the UN

Paul H. O'Neill   Chairman, ALCOA

Members

Paul A. Allaire   Chairman, Xerox Corporation

Jonathan Alter   *Newsweek*

Susan V. Berresford   President, The Ford Foundation

Derek Bok   former President, Harvard University

David L. Boren   President, University of Oklahoma

Michael J. Boskin   Hoover Institution, Stanford University

Bill Bradley   former United States Senator

Joan Brown Campbell	Director of Religion, Chautauqua Institution, former General Secretary, National Council of Churches of Christ
Henry G. Cisneros	President and COO, Univision Communications, Inc.
John F. Cooke	Executive Vice President for External Affairs, The J. Paul Getty Trust
Lee Cullum	Columnist, *Dallas Morning News*
Mario Cuomo	former Governor of New York
Douglas N. Daft	Chairman and CEO, The Coca-Cola Company
Thomas R. Donahue	AFL-CIO
Peggy Dulany	Chair, The Synergos Institute
Don Eberly	Chair and CEO, National Fatherhood Initiative; Director, Civil Society Project
Marian Wright Edelman	The Children's Defense Fund
Jeffrey A. Eisenach	President, Progress and Freedom Foundation
Dianne Feinstein	U.S. Senator
Jim Florio	former Governor of New Jersey
David P. Gardner	former President, The William and Flora Hewlett Foundation
John W. Gardner	Graduate School of Business, Stanford University
William George	Chairman and CEO, Medtronic
Peter C. Goldmark, Jr.	CEO, International Herald Tribune
Michael Goodwin	President, Office and Professional Employees International Union
William H. Gray III	President and CEO, United Negro College Fund, Inc.

David E. Hayes-Bautista	School of Medicine, UCLA
Bryan J. Hehir, S.J.	Dean, The Divinity School, Harvard University
Antonia Hernandez	President and General Counsel, MALDEF
Irvine O. Hockaday, Jr.	President and CEO, Hallmark Cards, Inc.
Charlayne Hunter-Gault	*The NewsHour with Jim Lehrer*
Frank Keating	Governor of Oklahoma
Robert D. Kennedy	Retired Chairman, Union Carbide Corporation
James T. Laney	President Emeritus, Emory University
Sara Lawrence Lightfoot	Professor of Education, Harvard University
Bruce Llewellyn	Chairman and CEO, Philadelphia Coca-Cola Bottling Co.
Richard G. Lugar	United States Senator
David Mathews	President and CEO, Charles F. Kettering Foundation
Elizabeth McCormack	Trustee, John D. and Catherine T. MacArthur Foundation
William J. McDonough	President, Federal Reserve Bank of New York
Dana G. Mead	former Chairman and CEO, Tenneco Inc.
Yolanda T. Moses	Board Member, The Ford Foundation
Diana Natalicio	President, University of Texas at El Paso
Harry Pachon	President, The Thomas Rivera Policy Institute
Deval L. Patrick	Vice President and General Counsel, Texaco
Robert D. Putnam	Professor of Political Science, Harvard University

Steven Rattner	Quadrangle Group LLC
Ralph Reed	former Executive Director, Christian Coalition
Robert B. Reich	Brandeis University; former Secretary of Labor
William D. Ruckelshaus	Chairman and CEO, Browning Ferris Industries
George Rupp	President, Columbia University
Henry B. Schacht	Chairman and CEO, Lucent Technologies Inc.
Arthur Schlesinger, Jr.	Department of History, City University of New York
Adele Simmons	Vice Chair, Chicago Metropolis 2020
Alan K. Simpson	Director, Institute of Politics, Harvard University
Edward Skloot	Executive Director, Surdna Foundation, Inc.
Theodore Sorensen	Paul, Weiss, Rifkind, Wharton & Garrison
Edson W. Spencer	former CEO, Honeywell Inc. & former Chair, Ford Foundation
Chang-Lin Tien	former Chairman of the Board, The Asia Foundation, UC Systemwide
Vin Weber	former Congressman
Frank A. Weil	Chairman, Abacus & Associates, Inc.
John C. Whitehead	Chairman, AEA Investors Inc
William Julius Wilson	John F. Kennedy School of Government, Harvard University
Michael Woo	Director of Los Angeles Programs, L.I.S.C.
Daniel Yankelovich	President, Public Agenda Foundation

About The American Assembly

The American Assembly was established by Dwight D. Eisenhower at Columbia University in 1950. It holds nonpartisan meetings and publishes authoritative books to illuminate issues of United States policy.

An affiliate of Columbia, The Assembly is a national educational institution incorporated in the state of New York.

The Assembly seeks to provide information, stimulate discussion, and evoke independent conclusions on matters of vital public interest.

American Assembly Sessions

At least two national programs are initiated each year. Authorities are retained to write background papers presenting essential data and defining the main issues of each subject.

A group of men and women representing a broad range of experience, competence, and American leadership meet for several days to discuss the Assembly topic and consider alternatives for national policy.

All Assemblies follow the same procedure. The background papers are sent to participants in advance of the Assembly. The Assembly meets in small groups for four lengthy periods. All groups use the same agenda. At the close of these informal sessions participants adopt in plenary session a final report of findings and recommendations.

Regional, state, and local Assemblies are held following the national session at Arden House. Assemblies have also been held in England, Switzerland, Malaysia, Canada, the Caribbean, South America, Central America, the Philippines, Japan, China, and Taiwan. Over one hundred sixty institutions have cosponsored one or more Assemblies.

Arden House

The home of The American Assembly and the scene of the national sessions is Arden House, which was given to Columbia University in 1950 by W. Averell Harriman. E. Roland Harriman joined his brother in contributing toward adaptation of the property for conference purposes. The buildings and surrounding land, known as the Harriman Campus of Columbia University, are fifty miles north of New York City.

Arden House is a distinguished conference center. It is self-supporting and operates throughout the year for use by organizations with educational objectives. The American Assembly is a tenant of this Columbia University facility only during Assembly sessions.

THE AMERICAN ASSEMBLY
Columbia University

Trustees

ARTHUR G. ALTSCHUL	New York
CHARLES BENTON	Illinois
BRADLEY CURRY, JR.	Georgia
DOUGLAS N. DAFT	Georgia
MEYER FELDBERG, *ex officio*	New York
DAVID R. GERGEN	District of Columbia
BILL GREEN	New York
KAREN ELLIOTT HOUSE	New York
B.R. INMAN	Texas
WHITNEY MACMILLAN	Minnesota
VILMA S. MARTINEZ	California
JOHN F. MCGILLICUDDY	New York
DONALD F. MCHENRY	District of Columbia
DAVID H. MORTIMER	New York
RAYMOND D. NASHER	Texas
GEORGE E. RUPP, *ex officio*	New York
DANIEL A. SHARP, *ex officio*	Connecticut
STEPHEN STAMAS, *Chairman*	New York
PAUL A. VOLCKER	New York
FRANK A. WEIL	New York
CLIFTON R. WHARTON, JR.	New York

Staff

Daniel A. Sharp, *President and CEO*
David H. Mortimer *Chief Operating Officer*
CECILE E. ALEXIS, *Manager*
DEBRA BURNS MELICAN, *Manager, Uniting America Series*
LISA K. BHATTACHARJI, *Program Coordinator for the COO*
LAURIE V. O'CONNOR, *Assistant to the President and CEO*
MITZI J. PELLE, *Programs Assistant*
JUNE C. SCOTT, *Financial Assistant*

Trustees Emeriti

WILLIAM BLOCK	Pennsylvania
WILLIAM P. BUNDY	New Jersey
CLIFFORD M. HARDIN	Missouri
SOL M. LINOWITZ	District of Columbia
KATHLEEN H. MORTIMER	New York
ELEANOR BERNERT SHELDON	New York
CLARENCE C. WALTON	Pennsylvania

Index